How to Hold an Umbrella

Edited by
Amanda Saint

ISBN eBook: 978-1-8380430-2-5
ISBN print: 978-1-8380430-3-2

Retreat West Books
retreatwest.co.uk

Contents

Foreword
Amanda Saint

AS ALWAYS, MY thanks go to the talented authors who submit each year for the Retreat West Short Story and Flash Fiction Prizes. The stories featured here are those that shine out the most from the many hundreds we read.

Many thanks to our judges – Angela Readman for the Short Story Prize and Meg Pokrass for the Flash Fiction Prize. It is not an easy job to decide between the 10 stories they get sent that have made it through to the final judging rounds.

And congratulations to all of the writers appearing here – it's great to see new names alongside those of writers whose work has been published in previous winners' anthologies too. The number of entries we receive is growing each year and the standard of writing we get to read is brilliant. There are so many talented writers in the short fiction world and we're honoured that we get to read so many of them.

The biggest congratulations go to our winners in each category – Emma Hutton for *Sal* in the Short Story Prize.

Angela said your story gave her goosebumps, and it did for all of us too. Emma also had another story on the shortlist, *My Kind*, which was published as *Sinkh♡le* in the *Outsiders* anthology from 3 of Cups Press. Thanks to them for kindly letting us reprint it here.

Sherry Morris is the deserving winner of the Flash Fiction Prize for her tiny story that says so much about domestic drudgery, *Treating the Stains and Strains of Marriage*. Meg Pokrass quite rightly highlighted among the many reasons it won its jaunty tone, dark humour and great use of metaphor. Characteristics that often shine through in Sherry's work, which we have had the honour of publishing several times so far.

Louise Farr was in second place in the short story category with *Whale Watching*, a gorgeous story of love, loss and finding your place in the world told through a unique and compelling voice. Third prize went to Jason Jackson for *Mess of Love*, an immersive tale of a relationship that was hard to predict an ending for. Kudos to Jason for appearing twice in this anthology as his flash fiction, *On the Death of a Friend*, was also shortlisted.

Second place winner of the Flash Fiction Prize was Niamh MacCabe with *Riverwater Cistern*, which captures the intensity of childhood friendships in beautiful language. Timothy Boudreau was awarded third prize for *Wormholes, Mushrooms, Silverfish* – a gritty, coming of age tale which enfolds the reader in the many senses.

We are really grateful to everyone who takes part in these prizes for sending us their words.

Amanda Saint
Publisher at Retreat West Books

Sal

Emma Hutton

SAL SPENT MOST of that summer in water. It seemed like
the safest place. There's a man out there, her mother had
said. Sal already knew. All the kids knew. They called him
The Bad Man. In two months, he'd left six girls to be
found with the rising sun, like milk bottles or newspapers
waiting in porches. He prised open windows and climbed
into their bedrooms. Girls like Sal. He didn't always kill
them but mostly he did. He pulled them out of their
rooms and onto the soft, wet grass where he twisted and
turned their bodies. But not The Bad Man, or the dead
girls, or the relentless rain stopped the kids racing from
their houses every morning to land the best spots at the
outdoor pool.

Since she could remember, Sal heard music in everything. The way people could see the colours of letters and
numbers, she could hear music. Everything gave off notes:
melodies twisted out of swimming costumes, dripped
down ice cream cones, slipped like prized coins out of

sweaty palms. Babies gave off the sweetest sounds. But since the day before her sixteenth birthday, the day the rain started to fall and didn't stop, everything and everyone sounded distorted. She could only hear the discordant breaking apart of notes sparked up into the air. There were no beats for her to rest on. She missed the music. It was her gut, her guide, the quiet voice that helped her figure out people and what to do with them. She stuck cotton buds into her ears. Pencils. Hair grips. But she couldn't fix what was broken in her and she couldn't stop the rain.

'He's so perfectly made. I can't believe you haven't done it yet,' Davey said. Davey was under the umbrellas the pool guys hauled out every morning and put back every evening. Sal never understood why they just didn't leave them out. It wasn't like the rain was going to stop. Not now. 'I would totally do that,' Davey said, wringing water from her hair. 'What are you waiting for?'

Davey was Sal's best friend and she was talking about Ru McManus. Ru was a kid that looked like a man in a film about saving the world. A broad-shouldered, boxed-out void you could fill with whatever made you feel better. Sal knew Davey had done it with a bunch of guys long before that summer started. Davey wasn't ashamed about wanting to be touched and to touch. Sal liked that about her. Davey gave out a solid, unwavering note like striking a bell. Or, she used to. Now there was just a space where the note should be.

'I am. We are. Tonight. His parents are away.'

'At last!'

'I told Maggie I'm staying at your house. Is that ok?' Sal asked.

'Sure, but I want all the details,' Davey laughed.

Sal looked and found Ru in the pool. Before the rain, he sounded like the curves of arcing waves rising up into the white expanse before falling back onto the beach. He was a careless, overflowing that she had avoided. Until now. Since the rain started and the music stopped, Sal had seen Ru in places she shouldn't have. She'd filled herself with the soft noises he made when she kissed him. When she pressed her finger to his lips and told him to 'shhh' but he couldn't and she didn't really want him to. She had tried to resist him but he was meant to be leant against. She wanted to carve him up and eat him. Fold him up like paper and stick him to the roof of her mouth. She loved him but knew if she fucked him too soon it would all be over and she wanted to play it out for as long as it could last. After it was done, guys like Ru didn't want girls like Sal. Davey taught her that. Guys like Ru who lived on tree-lined streets with back yards, who never had summer jobs, who were going away to school. They didn't want girls like Sal who had to work in the factory. Everyone in town called it The Factory. Her mother worked there. Davey was going to work there. It's where they all went. There, or to another town and another factory. Or the slaughterhouse. The Factory made capacitors that were used in computers, televisions, missiles and spaceships. It didn't matter that she didn't want to leave school yet, that she wasn't done learning about heroic couplets and what made the sky blue. She wanted those extra two years that the kids with new trainers and cars got. But that didn't matter. It was almost September. The unspoken deal was the kids got that last summer after school to do whatever they wanted and then they went to make chips at The Factory.

Sal wanted Ru to want her forever, that's why she made him wait. She wanted him to love her. But time was running out. He'd be gone soon and The Bad Man was still out there, looking for girls just like Sal. Fuck it, she thought. Better to have him now than risk ending up dead on the grass like those virgins, broken in endless ways except one.

'Where do you think he's gone?' Davey asked.

'Who?'

'The Bad Man. It's been weeks since the last girl.'

'Maybe he's on holiday.'

'On holiday?' Davey laughed. 'Maybe he's dead. Maybe he killed himself.'

'Why would he top himself?'

'Because he feels bad about killing those girls.'

'Maybe he doesn't like the rain. Maybe he's sick of it,

like the rest of us,' Sal said.

'Maybe he melted! Like the wicked witch of the west. Wait, is it east? West! Which one is it?'

'West. He's not dead. He's still out there.'

'Here,' Davey said, pulling two beers out of her backpack and throwing one at Sal. 'Shotgun.' Davey stabbed the can with a pocketknife she carried with her 'just in case' and handed it to Sal who pierced a hole. Together they held them up to their mouths and pulled the tabs. Warm beer exploded down their throats and across their cheeks. 'Want to come to mine for dinner?' Davey asked.

'Sure', Sal said, dropping the knife into her bag. Dinners didn't happen too often at her house. Maggie, Sal's mother, wasn't around much and when she was there was always a man on the scene. A man coming out of the bedroom, pulling his trousers up. A man in the shower blowing green rinds of snot onto the tiles for Sal to clean up later. A man on the stairs, counting each tread till he was outside her bedroom door.

Sal's mother was from the other side of town, across the fields where Ru lived. But when she hadn't been able to hide the baby growing inside her 16-year-old body and there hadn't been a good man to marry, her parents kicked her out. She'd got a job at The Factory, found a place to live and there she'd stayed. Maggie had always done whatever was easy and most of the time that was nothing. She always sounded like she was on fire, a constant burning out, expending oxygen, taking the good things out of the air.

When the sun started to fall they pulled jeans and raincoats over their swimming costumes and headed to Davey's house. Light bounced off the locked windows of all the houses that looked the same. Plants drooped and sad cats sat in windows, knowing that outside was worse than inside. The rain had fallen for so long that it had caused the ground to collapse in places. They appeared at the park, outside the skating rink, near the football pitch. The holes sucked in trees and roads and ice cream vans. When the earth took a sleeping baby from its own home, Sal had run a bath and stayed there until her mother forced her to get out. The hole sucked up a dog too and a newly installed eight burner gas range cooker. It was too deep to find the baby or the dog and it was growing. That poor baby, her mother had said, exhaling a line of smoke that sank into the carpet. The dead baby was enough to bump The Bad Man from the top of the news cycle.

At Davey's, they ate spaghetti with orange cheese grated on top, lying on their bellies, stretched out across the living room floor reading each other's palms. 'I see a little love but no babies and a short life,' Davey laughed, tracing her finger across the heaviest line on Sal's hand. It looked like a lightning bolt, branching up and out until it disappeared.

'Fuck you, man. I'm going to live to see them put you

in the ground!'

'We're going to live forever!'

SAL WOKE TO what sounded like a swelling wave and let it break across her. It was Ru. She was in his bed. She covered her ears and got up, walked to the window and before she pulled the heavy curtains she knew the rain had stopped. Her music was back.

'Hey.' Nothing. 'Hey!' She poked his shoulder and a green eye opened. 'I need to go.'

'I'll miss you,' he said, turning towards her. She climbed back onto the bed and straddled his chest. She thought about punching him between the clavicles but kissed him there instead. 'You will?' she asked. But he was asleep again and it didn't matter because it was over. She jumped off the bed, pulled on her clothes, grabbed her bag and walked out, shutting the door behind her.

The house was bigger than any she'd ever been in. She ducked in and out of endless clean rooms filled with books and pictures on the walls. She stopped in the biggest room and sat at a dresser in front of a window that looked out across the fields. She pulled opened the heavy drawers and inside found neatly packed rows of lipstick. She grabbed one in a gold case, popped the lid and ran the red stick over her lips. Sal stared at herself in the mirror. Exactly the same, she thought. She leaned over, kissed the glass, slipped the tube into her pocket and left.

Outside the sky was pink and white. It was a long, straight line to cut across the fields back to her house. The air was still wet but it wasn't as low to the ground. Sal heard flowers lifting their heads. The earth was drying out and she listened as it cracked and bent beneath her. She walked slowly, revelling in the return of the music. The sun was almost up. She'd forgotten her raincoat, not that she needed it but for a second she let herself imagine Ru bringing it to her. Telling her she should run away with him. As if, she thought and laughed. Then a noise came from behind her. She knew it was a man and it wasn't Ru. He was walking quickly, almost running. 'Hey! Hey!' the fast man shouted. He sounded like cogs turning, a meshing of gears before irreversible movement. She'd heard the noise before. In other men. In Ru too. They all gave off similar notes. If he killed her it wouldn't be so bad, she thought. She would never go to The Factory. Ru would never forget her. Maggie might even cry a little. She knew this man might not be The Bad Man but he was not a good man either. His noise was almost on top of her. A thundering of drums upon drums upon drums. She closed her eyes, reached into her bag and let the music beat across her body.

IT WAS FUNNY how much damage something so small

could do, she thought. She'd gone for his left thigh first. She'd read somewhere to attack the neck and thigh. Carotid and femoral. Then, when he was down on the ground, she moved to his neck. Each time the blade went in it made the sound of cheeks being sucked against teeth. He was making another noise from his mouth but she couldn't hear that. All she heard was the syrupy stuckness of an incomplete loop of motion. A stuttering. When she got to her feet, she saw his running shoes were double knotted, like his mother had tied them. His hair was a little too long at the sides and she saw the outline of a cross beneath his once white T-shirt. He didn't sound like anything now. Sal tapped him with her foot. He didn't move. She walked around to the other side, as if left and right might not be connected and kicked his arm. Out of his hand rolled the gold tube of lipstick she had taken from the dresser. She must have dropped it in the fields. She folded the blade of Davey's just-in-case knife, tucked it into her pocket and ran. The burr of her own sweet sound rose up into the sky. She ran from where Ru lived. She ran from her mother's hard hands. She ran from The Factory, past the football pitch, past the park, until her feet turned into knees and knees turned into palms. When she got to the pool, she climbed the fence and on the other side pulled off her clothes and shoes. She walked across the drying concrete and dived into the pool, pushing herself out into the water, away from the edges.

She opened up her hands and looked at her palms. The blood had dried out filling the lines that ran across them so they looked like strings of barbed wire.

As the sun rose, she listened to the soft, sweet notes that slipped from the blades of grass and climbed up and out of the fields between here and there. Between where she was and where she thought she belonged. Summer was over. She would go home, put on clean clothes and walk to work at The Factory. She would test the chips that go inside spaceships and missiles. She would think about how strange it was that people talked about space as if they weren't already in it. She would cling on to this rock, hurtling through the darkness until her line ran out.

Treating the Stains and Strains of Marriage

Sherry Morris

SHE'S IN THE supermarket – the laundry aisle to be precise. Today's special offer: colour catchers. 'Aha,' she says.

Reaching high, on tip-toe, using a mop from the next aisle, she knocks two rows of bright-orange boxes into her cart. Watches as twenty, thirty, maybe fifty postcard-size cartons tumble down. She races for the checkout, nearly running over an old lady. There's no guilt – old ladies are past their sell-by date. She still has shelf life.

In her kitchen, she tapes small white squares together into one large sheet with a fervour that would make an evangelical nod and shout 'Amen!' The cat pokes its nose in, smells danger, backs out. As she works, her lips recite the product's promises like a prayer.

Effective at all temperatures.

Prevents greying.

Prevents residual dirt redepositing.

At *Prevents run accidents*, she pauses. He'll need one too. Double-strength knowing him.

Inspired, she grabs Mr Muscle for an added bit of sparkle. It's not cheating. Potential double-coupon bonus: unwrapping to shapely calves, a toned stomach, banished bat wings. She reads the label. *Causes serious eye irritation.* She shrugs. Most husbands do. There's also *Avoid prolonged skin contact*, but that's what she craves. Decides it can't hurt any more than anything else in their marriage, applies liberally. Her skin prickles. She wonders if it's product or anticipation that makes her feel like a pincushion. She's glad a slow spin cycle is recommended. She'll hold on tight.

They're meeting at 3pm today.

She won't think about when, exactly, the heavy purples and greys sneaked under the door where the cracks were too wide. How some days black pooled on the ceiling, oozed down the walls, saturating her so completely she couldn't even slide out of bed.

She went crusty, rusty, musty. He asked what was wrong, but words and feelings clogged her heart. Not even a bottle of Drano had helped.

He went slimy and grimy, walking in gutters, slipping down drains, disappearing for weeks at a time. She no longer wanted his dirty hands on her. He moved out and dark blues swallowed her whole.

But the cat demanded to be fed, that she get out of bed. This and long soaks in fabric conditioner were the start. She marvelled at the crud that slid down the plughole.

'A vow is not just for now,' he'd said. They'd both been so light, so bright back then.

SHE RANG HIM while holding a bottle of Febreze. Suggested they meet in Soft Furnishings.

Now cocooned within her sheet, she waits for it to work. The cat arrives to check on her.

'Colour catchers have a money-back guarantee,' she says. 'That's not what I want back.'

The cat yawns – stares at her with clear glass-green eyes, begins his own methodical wash. She admires his agility, his self-care ability, the mix of colours in his calico coat. She remembers the rainbow she'd seen that morning. How its faint arc brightened the dark sky.

Whale Watching

Louise Farr

THE BLUE WHALE is the largest animal on earth. It has a tongue as big as an elephant and a heart the size of a small car. The arteries are so big that a human could swim through them.

When I was born I weighed the same amount as a bag of sugar. The nurse called me a dainty wee doll and said I was the spit of my Mother, who weighed less than a Swan feather. She named me after Anna Pavlova. 'My little pudding,' she laughed at my first ballet class, when my three-year-old knees were as soft as cookie dough. I listened to the plink plonk of the piano and tried to point my pink leather toes. That was when I could still see my feet.

She died when I was ten. She forgot to eat, so they put her in a hospital and gave her a plastic tube from her nose to her stomach. I wasn't allowed to visit after that. They tried everything but her heart stopped working. It shrank to the size of a sugar plum. They told me at school so my

Father didn't have to. He was making The Arrangements said The Nanny, who had already booked her flight back to New Zealand. I went up to my room and looked at the black and white photograph that I kissed every night. She glittered from a silver lake as I took a family sized bar of chocolate out of my backpack and bit down hard on it.

After the funeral, My Father took me to America on a DADDY DAUGHTER business trip. While he sat in air conditioned meetings, we went to a water park where the Whales rolled over like dogs and wagged their fins while everyone clapped. I cried big fat tears into my saltwater taffy. 'They like it here,' said The New Nanny, shoving a giant plush Dolphin in my face. 'They wouldn't do it if they didn't want to.' She bought me a hot dog in a soggy napkin and told me not to tell. I hated her, but I ate it anyway. A week later, a whale pulled one of the trainers into the water by her ponytail. 'See?' I said.

Sometimes I ate until my stomach hurt. My father sent me to Camp Olympus, where we dangled helplessly from high ropes and learned the correct portion size on a plate. I smuggled in Pop Tarts and Snickers bars that melted in my sleeping bag. After the Summer holidays, my bra bit into my sides and showed under my school shirt.

'Look at Pudding,' snickered the Mean Girls at school, flicking their manes. 'She's a little slut.'

I stopped going to school so my Father found me a

new one. It was progressive, he said, which meant it was for social rejects who knew how to ski. It didn't have a uniform or a chapel or a house system named after ancient scholars. I made friends with a girl who wanted to be a boy called Dorian and wore a silk smoking jacket to school. 'It's out of a book,' she explained. I failed every subject except Art. Once I told the school counsellor I wanted to be a Whale. She said it was understandable, considering the *family circumstances*, but she hadn't received any training for girls who identified as giant sea mammals.

I sketched Beluga and Orca and Humpback Whales. I drew dark silhouettes in tiny blue boxes of captivity. I made barnacled backs heave out of black water and breach themselves onto paper. I had a talent, said the art teacher, who used to be beautiful and smelt of Menthol cigarettes. She had long black hair and lidded eyes and didn't mention my Mother. 'You should consider art school,' she said.

My Father explained that art was a hobby, not a career. There was white spittle at the side of his mouth as he snapped at the waitress for another drink. Her smile was cut glass as I pretended I was at the bottom of the ocean. Sperm Whales can hold their breath for 90 minutes.

I left school at 16. I didn't tell him that the girls puffed out their cheeks and the boys offered blow jobs for not gobbing on me. Now I work in a call centre on an industrial estate, beside a 24 hour Drive Thru that reels me in like a bucket of chum. I have my own wooden box and a script that tells me what to say if a customer threatens to kill himself. We have a *high staff turnover* because not many people want to sit in a box and tell Bio Dads to cough up for their kids. They give me *dogs abuse* and tell me what they're going to do to me. 'That's not very nice,' I say. Sometimes the line goes dead.

My Boss likes me because I'm Well Spoken. He peels sardines out of a tin and tells me that he hasn't slept for four years. 'Don't have children,' he warns me, sucking a tail like a home sex video. He tells me his wife has piled on the pounds, put on the beef. 'I say nothing,' he confides, patting his stomach like a pet dog.

My colleagues call me Lady Muck and ask me to cover their shifts. My boss *turns a blind eye* because I have excellent timekeeping skills and I don't waste time on *chit chat* or *calls of a personal nature*. I don't *loiter in the staff kitchen area or have extended bathroom breaks. Staff should notify their team leader if they have any medical issues.*

Once I made Whale clicking noises without thinking and someone complained to our team leader. Probably Marian, who has crispy hair and plucks out her chin hairs at her desk. They gave me a card with a KARE-CALL number and advised me to swim with dolphins in my own time.

Whales don't eat much. Their mouths are giant sieves

that open and close. Some species can travel thousands of miles without feeding.

People say I have a pretty face, as if my head is the most acceptable part of me. My apartment has CCTV and security gates and a code that the delivery boys press to get in. My neighbours don't like that. They put notes through my door and a letter from the residents' committee. The Doorman says nothing. In his country the people have whale funerals and call them The Gods of the Sea. They don't squeeze them into swimming pools or turn them into soup.

The Doctor says *everything in moderation.* He asks me to describe an average day.

<u>My Day</u>

I adjust my headset and make my targets. I follow the script and I filter out the fake nails and bathroom tiles and *it's my day* weddings and useless husbands and anyone who cries in the toilet and *takes the job personally.*

Click Click.

It's Monday or Tuesday (who knows) when The Boss asks if he can Have a Chat. 'Bring your coffee,' he says ominously. I follow him into his office and there's a girl standing there with bright pink hair and red lipstick and half a dragon squeezing out of her cleavage. I can almost hear Marion saying *Another Circus Freak.*

'This is our new start,' he says.

'I have a name.'

The Boss is *Totally Scundered*.

'It's Doll,' she announces. Short for Dolly. NOT Dolores.'

'I'm Anna,' I say, surprising myself.

The Boss winces like he's just given himself a paper cut. He informs us that it's not a social club and herds us out with his hands, taking care not to touch us in case we sue him for sexual harassment. Men can't do anything these days, he says.

Doll makes a noise. 'What a dick,' she snorts to the closed door.

'He's okay.'

I try to *show her the ropes, tell her what's what*. She laughs when I tell her about the toilet breaks and the *penalties for poor performance*.

'Jesus, what a dive,' she says, flopping down at her desk. I watch her as she mouths on some lipstick and blots it on a post-it note. *Staff should be mindful of paper waste and the potential impact on the environment.*

I shrug.

'You don't say much, do you?'

She's bigger than me (how is that possible) but she doesn't care. Everything about her is bright and shiny as if she didn't get the memo about hiding under a rock. She has pink hair and red lips and a sundress with giant pineapples that shows off her bra straps and her sunburn. She fills up the room without even asking.

She offers me a stick of gum. 'Why are you making that weird clicking noise? You sound like a dolphin on drugs.'

I've never met another person like me.

Doll has 4.5k followers on her Instagram account and she once trended on twitter for being a bad influence. She uses *coarse language* and takes excessive toilet breaks but she makes all her targets and keeps The Boss happy, so he waves Marion away when she yaps like a terrier at a rabbit hole. He even treats us to a box of cakes in a white cardboard box that I lick in the kitchen when no one is looking.

'So, where do you go out?' she asks.

People stare at me in the streets, in supermarkets, in waiting rooms. In Summer, I sweat if I move and my thighs smack together like strangers on a one-night stand. Men lean out of cars and pull their faces into Halloween masks. They call me a fat bitch and a fucking whale while I fantasize about smashing their skulls with a flick of my tail.

'I don't go out much,' I say.

Whales beach themselves for a number of reasons. It could be the echo of a submarine or the buzz of a speedboat or ice caps, melting down the landscape. Sometimes they send out an SOS and the rest of the pod die too. Their chests rise and fall as humans wrap them in damp towels and bathe them in buckets of water. They suffocate under their own weight.

Doll takes me to the pub after work. She works in it sometimes, because *the bills don't pay themselves* and her boyfriend plays in a band but unfortunately he's not famous yet.

I don't tell her that my Father pays for everything.

She knows everyone in the pub and they yell out insults and she yells back above the Football match on the widescreen television and everyone is happy, even though their team is losing.

We get very drunk. I am sick twice in the disabled toilet and I accidentally pull the emergency alarm. I tell her about my dead Mother and how Whales sink to the bottom of the ocean when they die. She tells me about her nine brothers and sisters and how her Mum lost all her teeth on a faulty escalator and her Stepdad was secretly a drag queen until they caught him miming Celine Dion in her Mum's Shapewear and then they all supported him 100%.

'His stage name is Scarlet O'Hara,' she says. Her breath smells like cheese and onion crisps. 'He used to be a stripper in a club called Gherkins.'

The next day I get a taxi to work, although I should have booked a hearse. The Boss is in meetings all day, so I try to avoid Marian in case she smells my breath and files another complaint. Doll isn't there. I text her but there's no reply.

I take a call from a man who says he has a Samurai Sword.

He says I'll be sorry.

I hang up, although we're not supposed to. You can get into trouble for that.

That night I order extra toppings, side orders, double cheese. The doorman concentrates on his computer screen. A woman in the lift gives me a dirty look.

Afterwards, when my kitchen reeks of grease and fat and there are boxes and cartons on every counter, the buzzer goes again. I press it and her voice shatters my food coma.

'Open up Flipper,' she booms. She sounds drunk.

I don't want the neighbours assembling a lynch mob so I let her in. She's wearing a 50s prom dress scattered with citrus fruit, and her lipstick is smeared like a sad clown.

'We're going swimming,' she announces.

It's high tide. The sea is black and the seafront is quiet, with all the curtains shut. I can hear the waves swishing over the rocks and fizzing out at the edge of the sand and I wonder what's out there, deep in the ocean. Do Whales swim at night? They can't sleep, or else they would drown.

'Let's just paddle,' I suggest.

Doll snorts. 'What's the point in that?' She snakes down the zip of her dress and steps out of it like a Burlesque show. I don't know where to look.

'Now you.'

I haven't undressed in front of anyone for a long time, unless you count that time the girls at school got me in the toilets. My bra looks like an old fishing net.

'I won't look.'

I look around and there's no one about. The lights glitter and wink on the horizon. I could swim there tonight, if I wanted.

The water is freezing but I keep walking. I start laughing and Doll joins in. 'It's so cold,' we yell in high pitched voices. I bob in the water like a cork. The water is up to my waist and when I let myself fall, I am weightless like those men on the moon, the dancers that defy gravity, the Whales who breach to get a breath when the water is choppy and the spray sucks up all the air.

I lie on my back and float. I can see my toes and I'm not cold anymore. I could swim thousands of miles, cruise entire continents if I wanted to. I start swimming and I don't stop, even when I hear Doll screaming for me.

Click Click.

It was Doll who raised the alarm. They said that my ~~blubber~~ body fat saved me and I was inches from death until they wrapped me in foil and heaved me back to shore. I was even in the news, although they didn't mention my name or the reinforced hospital bed.

The psychiatrist asked me politely if I tried to drown myself and my Father left for a business trip at the other side of the world. I don't see Doll again. When I phone the pub, they say that she's Gone Away. The Boss phones and tells me that I have a disciplinary meeting when I get back.

I tell him that I'm going to rub off his scales with the back of my knife. Then I'm going to stick a knife in his tail end and pull out his guts. Then I put the phone down.

I clean the apartment. I type Whale Watching Trips into my phone, and there are people on a small boat with waterproof jackets, as if the sea couldn't swallow them up if it wanted to. I book two seats on the plane and I charge it to my Father's credit card. Then I get out my sketchbook and I draw a girl swimming, but she is not alone. There are dark shapes dancing in a slow waltz and the sea is a stage, an open call.

On the Death of a Friend

Jason Jackson

MY FATHER SAT in his chair as he told me there'd be learning in the loss, as there is in broken promises, as there is—sometimes—in lies.

My mother went shopping, bought me Shakespeare. 'For the challenge,' she said. 'For the difficult truths.'

My brother drove overnight, took me dancing, got me drunk, took me home. In the morning he was gone, leaving nothing, and I wondered if he'd ever been there at all.

Rachel wrapped us both in stiff new sheets, saying, 'When you're in a storm, all you can see is the storm, but when you're through it and it's gone you'll be glad of the feel of it in your blood.'

Elizabeth brought domestic cleaning products. 'An hour spent on your hands and knees on the bathroom floor is never an hour wasted,' she said, handing me yellow gloves with a sad smile.

Sophia took me walking to an overgrown grave. She

told me that at the end we must fall into darkness before we rise into light. The grass was wet on our boots, and the birds were singing and ridiculous in the trees. 'Everyone loses,' she said. 'And everyone is lost. You're no different to the rest of us.'

A stranger on a train, who watched me as I cried, told me to find the place where relief was hiding. *'It's in everything,'* he said, *'if you look hard enough.'*

Jamie gave me a photograph I'd forgotten, the three of us on a mountain, soaked by winter rain. 'What the hell were we doing there, anyway?' he said, laughing. 'And what the hell are we going to do now?'

Someone put their arm around me. Someone held my shaking hand. Someone said they didn't know what to say to me, so they said nothing else, and someone sent me home.

The mirror let me look at it.

The food let me cook it.

The television let me ignore it.

The flat let me walk from room to room to room.

The streets were wet; the traffic passed; some shops were open; some shops were closed. People I had never seen before walked by, and some of them were smiling at each other and some of them weren't, and in everything there seemed to be a message, and in everything—when I looked hard enough—there was nothing at all.

Until breathing. Until hard, bloody, biting, carpet-burn sex. Until the taste of shop-bought fish 'n' chips. Until a borrowed cigarette. Until a new song on the radio which sounded—a little at least—like an old one. Until new words on my tongue. Until North Sea swimming. Until heavy weights. Until the push of the wind made me laugh at its suddenness as I ran.

The world gave me all of this as it continued to turn. It still gives me all of this and more, because the sun still rises, bringing sunlight, and sometimes—still—it is warm.

Riverwater Cistern

Niamh McCabe

THE TINY SEAHORSES are the best find all summer. We find hundreds of them in the old toilet by the river, the one the fishermen have rigged up for when they spend all day looking over the bridge at shapes in the water. Wriggle-tailed and transparent, we watch them rising and falling in the cistern's river-water. When we come back with mashed leaves, they've disappeared. You say maybe they're gone on holiday, wouldn't you want to if you lived in a cistern. Anyway they're not seahorses, you say, they're shrimp, or baby midges. We flush the leaves. Heads together leaning over the cistern, we watch it fill up again until the rising water touches our hair.

We turn to snails, we always do. We make a family, put them in a box with a smaller box inside. We lay scutch-grass on top as blanket, or sky. Next day, they're gone too. We find one under the scutch but it turns out the shell's empty.

It's about time we looked after ourselves, you say,

would you like a bowl of cereal, Madame? Yes, Kind-Lady, I would, thank you. We strip dry seeds off a bush, put them in a tin, pour water over. We listen out to hear the snap-crackle-pop; you say you hear it, but I don't. We flush the lot and race to the bridge to watch the seeds spill out into the river through the fishermen's pipe. That's how we look after ourselves.

Then I'm away, on real holidays. So you go down to the bridge, all by yourself. And what do you do, all by yourself? Fall into the river and break your damn arm, that's what. How your bone must've snapped in half under the skin, did you hear it, like a wishbone, and you all alone. You couldn't get back up. You said you cried later, as if your brain had finally realised; too late for wishes.

When I get back, I see your poor broke arm, and cry at the breaking of a good bone, of your good bone. You won't let me sign the plaster because I wasn't by your side when you fell. And you say the seahorses came back while I was gone. You looked after them with just the one arm. They danced around like hundreds of baby ballerinas in the cistern, but went away again just when I came home, sank down invisible and secret through ground and back out into the river. They're probably in the sea by now. You say don't worry, they'll be back next year but I don't think so, not real seahorses, don't they need sea-salt.

The following summer, we'll go to the river and we'll

not look for seahorses. You'll bring me in under the bridge. You'll show me where you fell. We'll be barefoot, bare-legged in the water, skirts hitched into our knickers. I'll rub my hand over your arm, where your good bone has broken, and I'll feel nothing but softness.

My Kind
Emma Hutton

Dear Suzy,

Your heart is a sinkh♡le.

Love, You-Know-Who.

EVERY WEEK YOU-KNOW-WHO always ordered '*Suspiria-red*' roses for Suzy. The time they said to replace the 'o' in sinkhole with a heart I nearly lost my mind. I couldn't get over it. All that passion. I wished I was Suzy but I'm not. I'm Zola. I work at Flower Power, a floral concept store. It's not just flowers, we sell candles, and soap, and bags made out of old tyres. The owner is my best friend, Jules. That's how I got the gig. We've known each other since we were kids. We used to share baths when we were wee and cigarettes when we got older. Now we live together and Jules thinks I live in a fantasy world. She says I watch too many romance films but it's her that's always covered in a blanket on the sofa watching *The Philadelphia Story*. I work behind the till and write all the cards at Flower

Power. The cards are always about babies and baptisms and brides and dead bodies. And they're always from people who are sorry, or thankful or somewhere over the moon. People are so predictable.

I used to be a primary school teacher, but I lost my job after I bit one of the children. I said it then and I'll say it again: Don't put your finger in my mouth if you don't want me to bite it. I was always a biter. My mother said it started from day one and if I'd been born with teeth I would have 'had her tits off.' She used to say it was her fault because they had to cut me out of her. 'You got the taste for blood,' she would say, tucking me in.

Before I could walk, I tried to bite the dog and then the cat. But it wasn't until my teeth came in that I started to realise the damage I could do. Paresh Shah had to get his lip stitched back on. Bella Doone will forevermore have a full moon of teeth marks on her left shoulder. Sammy Maxwell lost a chunk out of his arm. I only wanted them to love me, but nobody wants a biter. I have to warn the people I'm with. Some listen better than others. They always like it at first, teeth on skin. But that soon fades.

Dear Suzy,

I'd like to see you at the bottom of the sea.

Love, You-Know-Who.

'Zola, have you thought that this You-Know-Who might actually be crazy? Like, crazy-crazy.' Jules is sat on the living room floor cutting up old Christmas cards so she can turn them into new Christmas cards. She likes to make new things out of old things. She's so thrifty.

'He's not crazy. He's passionate.'

'How do you even know it's a he?'

'I just do. I have a feeling and that feeling is that he might be the right person for me.'

Jules hums. She's not convinced about my obsession with You-Know-Who. She likes to say she enjoys the idea of love, but she understands the reality of it. She's been seeing The Doctor for almost a year but refuses to call her that. Instead she says The Doctor is 'my little friend' like she's Al Pacino in *Scarface*. The first night they fucked she asked The Doctor to check her moles. Jules is very pragmatic and the smartest person I know. She wears a locket with a picture of herself inside. The picture is her as a six-year-old in overalls and white star shaped sunglasses. It reminds her to give herself a break, to be kind to the little her. See – she's so smart! To be fair, it's the oldest trick in the therapist's book: *Would you be this hard on the little you?* Jules sucks on the locket when she thinks, which is a lot. I worry about her teeth. The Doctor, Jules' girlfriend, thinks she should put a picture of her in the locket. She even gave her a passport photo put in it. Ugh. I try not to hate The Doctor.

I've been to all kinds of therapists since biting Paresh's lip off in the playground. I even went away on a 'retreat' for a little while. I've sucked on endless lollies and spat out enough gum to cover as much sky as I can see. I tried biting myself but it wasn't the same. My last therapist told me my biting is a confused kind of intimacy and I should 'find my kind.' I looked online and it turns out 'my kind' is the kind that wants to do more than just bite.

The last real relationship I had was with Substitute Teacher. He said Edith Wharton was his favourite writer, but he'd never even heard of *Ethan Frome*. He wrote me rhyming poems about rollercoasters and spiders. He rhymed love with glove and dove. I was allowed to suck at his underarm but one time I went for his neck and he pushed me off the sofa. 'No neck,' he said and wagged his finger. After the biting incident with the child he said I couldn't be trusted and I was secretly grateful to Clementine Ridley and her desire to stick fingers in open holes. We had one last night together and in the morning I bit all the rubber buttons off his remote controls and spat them out the window.

I got 'back out there' pretty quickly because that's what I was supposed to do. Jules told me I should bide my time, but love waits for no woman. I met Salami Man on a dating app. He was my only match. I'd decided to go with honesty as the best policy. My bio read: *I don't like to fight, I like to bite.* Everyone's always telling each other to be themselves. So, I was trying to be myself. I wanted someone to sink my teeth into. We went for drinks and after he asked if we could stop off at a corner shop. We did and he bought a pack of salami. He ate the whole thing himself with his hands and didn't offer me any. In bed, I bit his lip and his wrist but then he said, 'that's enough.' 'What about my bio?' I asked as he put his salami-smelling hand over my mouth. While he slept, I got dressed and closed the windows before taking a little chunk of out his backside. I knew he'd be a screamer.

Dear Suzy,

I hope you get fucked by a bear.

Love, You-Know-Who.

Turns out You-Know-Who owns a paint shop. I know this because I found his name on the order system and then I googled him. Up popped Splatter, a fancy paint shop he owned. There was a picture of him inside a drawing of a paint tin. He had a beard and he looked quite tired. I also found some pictures of him with a woman with dark hair cut into a square. In most of the photos she is wearing red lipstick and clinging onto him with one hand and making a fist with the other. I wondered if she was Suzy with the sinkhole heart. She looked like a Suzy.

SPLATTER DOESN'T SMELL like paint. It smells like rat traps and the antiseptic wipes you rub across children's scraped knees. It's not as fancy as it looks on the website.

'I can't believe you dragged me out of bed on a Saturday for this. This is legit stalker territory. You're Meg-Ryan-in-Sleepless-in-Seattle levels of bananas right now.' Jules is sucking her locket. 'We should not be here.'

'Shhh. Don't you want me to find 'my kind', Jules?'

Jules rolls her eyes, picks up a card full of yellow squares and fans her face with it. 'My little friend wants you to stop biting me.'

The Doctor. I hate the fucking Doctor with her stupid shiny hair and always taking my space on the sofa. She's always lining up tins in the kitchen cupboard and sighing when I walk into a room.

I pick up a card covered in white squares and stare intently at one called Stone White. I don't really bite Jules. Not anymore. Not since we were teenagers. I suck. Mostly the inside of her elbow when we're watching murder shows. Occasionally she gives me her ankle. Sometimes I forget myself and nip a little. Sometimes I think she lets me forget myself. I always ask if she wants to bite me back, but she never does.

'She found teeth marks on the last mole inspection.'

But I was so careful. I wonder if Jules is lying.

A man appears next to me gesturing at the card full of white squares that I'm now waving in front of my face.

'Looking for something in white?' It's You-Know-Who with his beard wearing a plaid shirt and jeans. He smiles and I look at his wrists and then at his mouth. I feel sick. Sick in a good way. He looks like a detective that never gives up. The one that will find your dead daughter or die trying.

'Do you have white? Not this Stone White or Caspar White. Just white-white.'

'What about Stalker White?' Jules whispers.

'We can do white-white,' he smiles. 'A matt finish?'

I nod.

'One tin?'

I nod.

'OK, let me get that for you,' he says, walking off. 'See you up at the till.'

'He smells weird. Like that blue ice cream we used to eat when we were kids. I don't like it.'

'Jules, don't.'

'Zola and the weird guy sitting in a tree…'

Jules doesn't like anyone I like. She never has. Maybe he does smell a bit weird but so what. Everyone smells weird now. It's all wet concrete, a rose in Chernobyl, trapped sunlight in an undiscovered monk's cave. The last perfume I bought, the woman at the counter described it as: 'Imagine you've escaped from the witch's oven in Hansel and Gretel. You are running. You are finally free.' It smells like burning hair, gingerbread and trees.

I leave Jules with the yellows and head for the reds.

'Red?' He appears out of nowhere. Conjured. 'It's a tricky colour,' he says, looking at the card full of red squares in my hand. 'People are afraid of it. Most use it as a one-wall colour in the kitchen or for a kid's playroom. Are you afraid of it?'

'I'm not afraid of red,' I say and point to one I think looks like the colour of my insides split open. Red roses. Almost neon. 'This one reminds me of something.'

He leans over for a closer look. 'That's Red Stallion 2. My favourite. Would you like a tester?'

'*Suspiria*.'

'Excuse me?'

'It reminds me of the colour of the blood in *Suspiria*. The film.' I look at him and wait for something to happen. He closes his eyes for a second and I imagine what's behind them: red-red blood dripping off a foot, sliding down a duck egg blue wall, tangled in hair, washing down a plughole.

'Would you like to go for dinner sometime?'

ON TUESDAY A woman with a square haircut comes into the shop. She's got a fistful of red roses. Jules has gone to pick up lunch so it's just me. Me and Suzy. Me and Suzy in the shop. She pushes a card across the counter. It's the one I wrote last week. I pick it up.

Dear Suzy,

I dreamt you were dead and it was wonderful.

Love, You-Know-Who.

My handwriting really is beautiful. We don't value penmanship enough these days. Fucking computers. You can see where the nib has touched the card, the rise of fall of the ink linking everything together like stars in a constellation. A perfect tumult flowing like champagne from a mountain of George Best glasses. A tamed Twombly.

'Excuse me.' The woman's face has turned as red as the flowers.

'How can I help?' I act cheerier than usual.

'I need you to stop sending me these flowers.'

'Oh. Is there something wrong with them?'

'It's not the flowers, it's the man who sends them. It's my ex. He sends those horrible cards.' She points at the card in my hand.

'Oh, I'm sorry. We thought it might be a lovers in-joke.'

'It's not a joke.' She starts shaking the flowers in her tight little fist. 'He's insane.'

'Insane?' Potato, potahto.

'He rowed us out to a tiny island in the middle of a lake and left me there. He said if I loved him as much as he loved me I would find my way across the water back to him. There were swans.'

I think I like You-Know-Who even more. I want to tell Suzy that true love isn't meant to be easy, that it's a battlefield. It's a test. But I don't say anything because she clearly does not understand love or romance. Poor Suzy, doesn't she know you've got to fight for a love that's real.

'I was out there all night. Waiting for someone to find me.'

'Can't you swim?'

'It was November.'

'So, you really didn't love him?'

Her mouth opens and I want to lean across and shut it before drool comes out. 'If you don't stop sending these fucking flowers I will go to the police.'

She launches the flowers across the counter and storms out the door that Jules walks in. 'Suzy with the sinkhole heart?'

'That's the one.'

Jules flips the sign on the door and locks it. 'What did she say?'

I tell her about the boat and the lake and watch as Jules' eyes get bigger.

'OK, there's no way you are going out with that maniac tonight. No way. You hear me?'

I tut. Jules hates my taste. 'Suzy's exaggerating and that's her loss. He was trying to prove how much he loved her.'

'That's your takeaway from her story? That he loved her? Jesus Christ, Zola.'

'Don't worry about it. You met him. He was fine.'

'I saw him for one minute and he didn't seem like anything. Please don't go tonight. I'll ditch my date with The Doctor and we can stay in. We can watch *You've Got Mail.*

'I need to find my own Doctor, Jules. Don't you want that for me?'

'If he ends up murdering you it's your own fault.' She drops a cheese sandwich on the counter for me and walks out to the back, kicking a bucket of dahlias as she goes.

'YOU'VE GOT TINY little teeth. Perfect little squares.' You-Know-Who reaches out but doesn't touch my face.

'Thank you, I'm a grinder.'

'What do you do?'

'I work at Flower Power. It's my best friend's shop.' He doesn't flinch. 'It's a floral concept store.'

The waiter comes and tells us the specials in a sonorously deep Italian accent that might be fake. You-Know-Who says he wants the seafood pasta and I should have it too.

'You know, I really think women should just be themselves.'

'Oh, me too,' I say, touching my face to feel for some

part that might have fallen away.

He looks between my eyes. 'Make-up. I think most women are much prettier without. Don't you.'

In the bus on the way here I had drawn black lines across my eyes and made my cheeks pinker than they usually are. I thought I looked better. I knew I did.

'Of course,' I say, picking at the red polish covering my thumbnail. It comes off in one piece that I fold over on itself until it disappears.

When the food comes it's full of mussels that look like sun-wasted buoys and slippy squid rings that I swallow down whole. He cuts his spaghetti with a knife and fork. I wind the strands around my fork and look at him, smiling. We don't speak for a very long time and I wonder if this is a test I might be passing. Eventually the waiter clears our plates and pours out another glass of wine from the bottle of white You-Know-Who chose without looking at the list.

'I don't like to talk during dinner. I think it's a sacred time, don't you?'

I start to wonder what I think but before I can get anywhere all the waiters in their white shirts are singing and one approaches our table holding two tiny plates. On each sits a square of chocolate cake with a shiny pink rose.

You-Know-Who leans over, 'Smile and play along. When I booked I told them it was your birthday. You get free cake for birthdays. Buon compleanno!'

'My birthday's not until June,' I say when the waiters leave.

'Don't you want your cake?'

'I don't like cake.'

'But I got it for you. You should eat it. Go on,' he says, pushing the little plate towards me. 'Do it for me.'

Cake reminds me of children's parties that I either ruined or didn't get invited to. 'I'll take it home for my friend.' Chocolate is Jules' favourite but she's not that picky.

You-Know-Who scowls when I ask the waiter to wrap it up for me. His face turns red when the cake is brought back to me parcelled in a tin foil swan and I remember the red-faced woman in the flower shop.

'I didn't order cake for your friend, I ordered it for you. If you don't want it, I'll take it back.' He reaches for the swan's neck but I bat his hand away. At first I think he's playing. But then does it again and again, eventually we're both standing up and he's trying to wrestle the swan away from me. The next time he lifts his hand, I grab it and put it to my mouth. I bite the soft fleshy bit between the thumb and forefinger. It's a good bit. I get carried away and tear a little. When he starts to howl I let go and make a run for it, out the door and down the dark street. I flag down the bus that's almost pulling away, the silver swan must have got the driver's attention. 'Thanks for stopping,' I pant and smile.

'You've got something in your teeth, love.'

'THE DOCTOR DUMPED me.' Jules is sat on the sofa watching Meg Ryan stood on top of the Empire State Building. 'She said I was hard work.'

'Fuck her,' I say, dumping the tin foil swan in her lap. 'You're not hard work.'

'You swear?'

'I swear,' I say, slumping down beside her. 'You're the easiest person I know.'

'Fuck you.' She punches my arm. 'What about my moles?' she asks, unwinding the swan's battered neck and pushing the square of cake into her mouth.

'I'll check your moles.'

She shifts around on the sofa and swings her legs onto my lap. 'I'm sorry about fighting earlier. You can go out with whoever you want. I just worry about you.'

'Well You-Know-Who is definitely not The One.'

'Was it bad?' Jules sucks her locket.

I nod.

'Maybe there isn't a One.'

'There's no my kind?'

Jules shrugs. 'Maybe we should stop watching these stupid films.'

'Maybe.'

'Here.' She raises her right ankle off my lap and offers

it to me. I take it in my hands and suck until my cheeks are sore and I start to feel good.

'Want to try?' I ask dropping her ankle back onto my lap. I extend my arm and she lifts my wrist to her mouth. She closes her eyes and sucks.

'It feels nice.'

'You can use your teeth. If you want.'

She bites gently at first, then harder until the red comes. It runs fast, dripping down the length of my arm.

She releases my wrist and smiles a red smile.

Finally, someone who is my kind.

Wormholes, Mushrooms, Silverfish

Timothy Boudreau

YOU WERE FOURTEEN, porcelain-boned, powder-pale, of course you liked cool and shadowed places, with a scent of earthworms, and book piles where lived silverfish. In your basement the air was mushroom-musty, the back half unfinished, crumbling away into dirt and darkness. Along the wall two bureaus filled with books. Austens and Brontës, Harlequins and Silhouettes, Asimov, Bradbury. The glossy covers cool and damp, the pages inside yellow-brown, like graham crackers softly dusty to the touch.

On summer days when you were sent down for badminton racquets, you stole a moment to read a few paragraphs, kneeling beside a bureau with a book in your lap. Glanced at your stepbrother's poster, Cheryl Tiegs in a burnt orange bikini. Read a snatch of a Harlequin sex scene, with collarbone kisses and hardening nipples.

If you heard someone calling you dropped the book

and closed the bureau drawer.

'What's going on Mitchell?' your mom asked.

Stepping out the basement door into the bright sunshine you winced into the light. 'Nothing. I found them.'

'For fuck's sake,' your stepbrother said.

'I found them didn't I?'

'It takes you forever to do anything.'

'Leave him alone Keith,' your mom told him.

You crossed the lawn to the badminton net through the sun, thinking of furtive caresses, basement mushroom kingdoms. On one side of the net were your stepfather and stepbrother, on the other you and your mother—so it wouldn't be a fair match. There was no shade in this part of the yard and the sun hurt your eyes.

What was the final score, 21-6? Your stepbrother slapped the final shot in your direction; when you swung and missed, it bounced off your forehead.

Keith: 'What an idiot, you're useless.'

Everyone went in separate directions, to the A&P, up the block for an ice cream, you had no idea. You grabbed your Walkman, notebook and pen and sat in the shade. Pressed play: K-tel's *After Hours*. Wrote about a boy in English class, with a pout, freckles and twitching hips; with hazel eyes, a cowlick and icy deadpan. A fantasy world like stepping through a funhouse mirror. Wormholes, transformations, otherworldly visitors, apparitions.

They didn't know you existed.

That night Keith was staying with a friend, so you'd have the bunkbed to yourself. In the bathroom changing into your bedtime sweats, you overheard your mom and stepdad watching a Movie of the Week while discussing your future.

'Stop it, he doesn't know he's like that.'

'He doesn't know how to *talk* to people.'

'He has time to learn.'

In bed at last you wrapped yourself with your own puny arms. Dreamt of the being who would in time find all of you, your odd shape and speech, strangely alluring. Dreamt of silverfish constellations, deep-sky objects, spiral and yellow elliptical galaxies, young star clusters. Dreamt of another's elbows and knees, as well as lips, collarbone and nipples. Dreamt of the bliss of nestling with them, sharing your bodies' salt, musk, words, breath.

Cuba

Bruce Meyer

THE SMELL OF Cuba is beautiful. Every place has its own smell. London, for example, has a different smell than it used to have. It was unmistakable as you stepped off an airplane and lined up in the Customs and Immigration Hall at Heathrow. London had the aroma of beer, heavy lubricating grease like the kind they use on escalators, and diesel exhaust from cabs. It doesn't smell the same now. It has changed.

I would wait to inhale New York until I got down around 11th Street in Tribeca before it got to be trendy. New York smelled of saltwater, dank basements, car exhaust, and unfiltered cigarettes. Chicago always had a note of feed grain and animal offal. Austin smelled of dust and heat. Heat has a smell. It is dry. You feel as if the inside of your nose is slowly being cooked, and beer, though not English real ale like I detected in London. I can close my eyes and you can put me on a plane and when I land I can tell you where I am.

Havana is my favorite. It smells of the car exhaust I knew from my childhood before emission controls became standard in North America. Rum, a sweet note hiding in the background, but hard to detect. And cigars. Cigars everywhere. That's where I developed my love of what my friends call the most disgusting habit in the world. Cohibas. Cohibas and liquor. I can almost imagine I am in Cuba when I open a bottle of Jack Daniels. There's smoke in there somewhere, which is why I have gone to great lengths to recreate the smell of Cuba. I mustn't forget the note of ocean salt. That's there, too.

My wife left me because I said she smelled like Quebec City, like stone that is cold even in late spring. My dog gets wet in the rain. She's stonily metallic, and sometimes I smell my wife on her, not as she was but as she became. A garrison city. The cold hard smell of a clear day when you look east along the St. Lawrence and you see all the way down to where fresh water meets the sea. But you don't smell fresh water in Quebec City. Everything smells like my wife when she said we were over.

I told her she was the stony silence on the seaway, as Leonard Cohen called it. It is the smell of a worn-out relationship, the personal ramparts meant to keep invaders at bay.

That's why I smoke cigars and drink heavy black rum. I want to remember Cuba. I want to smell the saltwater on her skin, a Cohiba between my fingers as she lay down glistening beside me. The oddly out-of-place aroma of coconut suntan lotion after it is salted by the sea.

I want to tell myself I haven't forgotten what love is because I can still smell it, though each reminder is slowly killing me.

The Black Hole of Westminster

Rhys Timson

ONE DAY IN December, Big Ben wasn't there. Its absence was noticed a few hours before dawn – rough sleepers and red-eyed clubbers staring up at the space where it should have been and seeing nothing but the night sky.

TV crews swarmed in with their vans and boom mikes, and helicopters filmed the absence from above. A square hole of earth was all that remained, even the foundations had disappeared up the magician's sleeve. As is the way with these things, the government called a COBRA meeting. There had been no explosion and there were no pieces of Gothic facade floating in the Thames, so terrorism – at least of the conventional kind – was ruled out. Security cameras captured the more awful truth: at two minutes to five the tower was there, a second later it was not. The prime minister talked about an 'anomaly', as if that meant something.

A lot of people assumed it was a joke, a stunt for a TV show – perhaps a comeback for David Copperfield. There were those who blamed aliens, while the more religious noted it as a demonstration of the illusory nature of existence. There were some who said the clock tower had never been there at all. They called them Ben-denialists, or Bendies for short. We all had false memory syndrome, they said. Photographs had been doctored. How could an entire clock tower blink out of existence?

But people soon got on with their lives, as people do. The TV crews went away and were replaced by construction companies. The government launched a competition to design a new tower, the whole thing financed by Doha. The deal was all but signed when the discovery was made.

A research team investigating the nesting habits of the Peruvian beagle bird spotted it three months after the vanishing – Big Ben that is – vine-crept and green with moss, deep in the Amazon rainforest. The hands of the clock were stopped at two minutes to five.

The operation to bring it home was immense. Hundreds of Peruvian labourers; a 150-metre crane; a giant, wheeled sled; a 70-mile track of rainforest cleared to provide a path; two indigenous tribes displaced. No-one knew where the money came from, no-one asked.

Street parties were held to welcome the errant timepiece home. Crowds lined the riverside as it sailed up the Thames, recumbent on a purpose-built barge rented from a Chinese shipping firm. People crowded the route from Gravesend to Embankment, waving plastic flags and cheering the pootling progress of time's missile. The news channels covered nothing but, titling their programmes things like *Ben's Journey, Ben's Coming Home* and *Ben's Big Adventure*. The tower was hoisted back in place to a nationwide cheer.

Little or no attention was paid to the physicists.

For a while, the debacle seemed like a boon. Tourism was four or five times higher than usual that year, and everyone flocked to Big Ben for a selfie outside the wandering tower. Get your pictures while you can, the tourism officials said. Who knows where Ben will be off to next?

The money that came in was almost enough to make up for the expense of the rescue operation, and the incident seemed destined to become just another funny story, a historical quirk. An inquiry was launched, but the report wasn't expected for many years. It's just one of those things, people said, like the Bermuda Triangle, we'll never know why.

But the following spring, St.Paul's disappeared.

This sparked a greater anxiety, particularly when it became apparent that the dean and several other staff were inside at the time. The disappearance had happened in the early hours of the morning, but witnesses reported looking out the windows of their night buses and seeing the cathedral there one minute, then gone the next.

People started to pay attention to the physicists then. Everyone had an opinion on wormholes, black holes, white holes, and Einstein-Rosen bridges. The upshot? According to the dominant theory, the earth was passing through a series of mini space-time anomalies, and London just happened to be at the epicentre. The situation had nothing, *note nothing*, to do with the Large Hadron Collider. If they could track the tachyon trails, the scientists mused, they could identify where on the planet St.Paul's and its occupants had disappeared to.

The Monument was next, in the middle of a rainy day in April. Workmen on the nearby construction site said the same thing as the night-bus travellers – they looked once and it was there, they looked again and *poof.* A crisis meeting was called, scientists from around the world flocked to London to attend a conference. Meanwhile, St.Paul's was spotted in deepest Siberia, the corpse of the dean frozen solid in the tundra about a mile beyond the front gate. Buckingham Palace relocated to Argentine Patagonia, the Tower of London to the backwaters of Kerala. One by one, London's tourist attractions blinked out and reappeared scattered across the globe. Then the financial centre was hit, the top of the Shard suddenly poking out of the Gulf of Akbar, the Gherkin sliding to a shattering crash down the north slope of the Eiger. Most of the buildings were unoccupied, but some late-night workers and cleaners found themselves radically transposed, the dark beyond their windows suddenly switched for the searing sunlight of the other side of the globe.

There was panic. People started to refuse to go to work, even to leave their homes. Tourism nose-dived, preachers predicted the end times. But then a MIT professor theorised that the wormholes were only affecting buildings with a strong psycho-sociological significance, giving new credence to the anthropic principle, but raising the question of just how important an object would have to be to vanish. Another physicist offered a supplementary hypothesis based on quantum mechanics – that the buildings could not move while their location was being observed.

For a while, that breakthrough stabilised things – while also solving Europe's unemployment problem. Tens of thousands of people were hired as 'watchers', employed simply to look at buildings. Since no-one could be sure how significant a place had to be for it to be a target, even the lowliest of offices and most obscure of sights paid people to eyeball their locations. Since one second of non-observance was all it took, teams of watchers had to be hired for each job, with round-the-clock cover essential and asynchronous blinking a fine art. Training colleges were established, employment agencies set up. Some of the more prestigious firms even started to compete to have the highest number of watchers on the payroll – the more observers, the more important a building had to be.

Things stopped going missing, but the buildings that had already disappeared proved hard to recover. Buenos Aires had no intention of returning the Queen's place of residence, at least not without swapping it for Las Malvinas. Delhi dragged its heels on the Tower of London, Russia said *nyet* on giving back St.Paul's. But while all this was going on the research teams had been busy on a more technical solution.

And that was how the Taj Mahal came to be sitting at the end of the Mall. A team from the UK's top new physics lab had tried to pull the Tower of London back the way it went with a reverse tachyon beam, but their calculations had been off. New Delhi protested, but in trying to return the Taj the team only succeeded in dumping 40,000 cubic metres of the Thames onto the Indian capital. The Indians threatened legal action, but a second effort to put the Taj back where it came from caused the accidental theft of the Agra Palace. London refused to take the blame; British scientists were trying to solve a global problem, they said, the wormholes were a force of nature. But already a rapaciousness was setting in.

A frozen St.Paul's was returned to its rightful place in the capital's skyline, but with it came the Bolshoi Theatre. Buckingham Palace was transferred to a new site near Windsor, but took the Cathedral of La Plata along for the ride. The 'accidents' started to multiply as London brought home its places of interest. Soon a person could look down from Parliament Hill and see the ornamented eaves of the Forbidden City, the ancient dome of the Hagia Sophia, and through the hazy smog the red glow of Uluru.

The rest of the world was outraged. But by that point it was too late.

London's physicists had had years to practise their art on the wormholes, had perfected the process of opening and closing them at will, pushing objects along tachyon trails to anywhere they desired. Planes, tanks, aircraft carriers – even ICBMs – could be picked up and deposited wherever London pleased. Moscow was the first, and the last, to find this fact out.

London lived that way for several years, as the centre of the world – picking up whatever it wanted, putting down whatever it tired of. The technology was quickly commercialised, and the City became a global logistics hub – sending goods as well as people anywhere the companies were paid to do so. They were indiscriminate – drugs, firearms, fissile materials – nothing was out of bounds.

When it all started to go wrong, it started small. Favourite mugs went missing, socks lost their partners, car keys disappeared. In the early months, the dissolution was imperceptible from the randomness of ordinary life. A strange epidemic of forgetfulness seemed to settle over the city, with everyone struggling to find their phones, their wallets, their bags. Then larger items started to go – cars, televisions, computers – and the MET was inundated with reports of theft. Only when the objects became less valuable did it begin to settle in. Trees, paving stones, walls, windows, everything started to vanish. Some people fled, leaving London for the cities of the north, taking the next flight back to Spain or Greece. But trains and planes disappeared too, as did whole streets of ordinary houses, as did people. There were riots, but even as the gangs looted designer trainers from smashed shop windows the boxes they held vanished from their hands. The fabric of space-time had been cut and stitched up too many times, now it was torn. People collapsed on the streets as their lungs or their hearts were drawn along invisible trails to reappear, still pulsing and bloody, over some distant part of the world's surface. But most things never re-emerged, lost as they were to some more distant point in the universe, some deeper rabbit hole.

The process accelerated rapidly, and within a few days there was no-one living within the M25. As the last Londoners blinked out of existence all that was left for them to see were the monuments and the skyscrapers – the sites of psycho-sociological significance – somehow anchored now against the gravitational pull of the wormholes. A row of tombstones in acres of anonymous dirt.

And still there, dead centre where it all began, was the black hole of Westminster, holding steady over the gutted capital, forever gurgling like a happy drain.

National Order

Helen Eccles

THE NAVY-BLUE TRANSIT van slipped quietly through the darkness into the space outside 22 Highland Road. It reminded Martin of the private ambulance that came to the Nursing Home around the corner whenever there was a death. He suspected, that perhaps, it was in a similar line of work.

'It's them, I think. I'll go wait by the door,' he called out to his wife.

Clare sat at the kitchen table, her fingers clasped tightly around a mug of un-sipped tea, knuckles protruding like bony white ball bearings.

Martin placed the palm of his left hand on the screen the clean-cut young man held out to him.

'All authorised Mr Carter,' said clean-cut with a smile. 'Here's the tablet. It's fitted with a tracker. Don't take it anywhere outside your house, don't try tamper with it and don't show it to anyone other than your wife. Follow all the instructions precisely. I'll be back to collect it within ninety minutes.'

FOUR DOORS DOWN, at number 14, Nicky Nicholls snatched the limp envelope lolling like a damp brown tongue from the letterbox.

'Nothing good comes in brown envelopes,' she muttered, shuffling back to the kitchen. She pondered whether to open the letter before or after her breakfast. Neither, with breakfast, food would sweeten whatever it was about. And besides, it would give her something to moan about when she got to work. Nicky always looked for the positives in life.

Two slabs of bread erupted from the toaster, their singed edges scraping against the metal grills. Eating was the most pleasurable thing in Nicky's life, followed by smoking and drinking. Saliva pooled under her tongue. She loaded her knife with butter, spreading it thickly over the toast before sliding it into her wide-open mouth and biting down into the soft warm cloud of cheap white bread. It had to be cheap. It had to be white. She took another bite before she had swallowed the last and golden rivulets seeped out of the corners of her fleshy, slack mouth.

BACK AT NUMBER 22, Martin and Clare stared at the blank screen as instructed. Clare perched on the edge of her seat, shuffling uneasily. She patted for the cat to jump into her lap.

'Let's book a last-minute holiday after we've done this,' Martin said, daring to look away from the screen for a moment, daring to think life was still normal just for a last few seconds.

'Yes, why not? The decorating can wait can't it?' Clare replied, playing along.

'Facial recognition complete. You have 1 secure message,' a synthetic voice said. It was the end of normal.

Their heads snapped round like soldiers called to attention.

Sender: Department of Citizen Compliance

31 October 2029

Please enter your security code _ _ _ _ _ _

'S.7.4.A.U.X,' Martin said. Clare's hand trembled as she tapped it in.

A white clock against a blue background flashed onto the screen, it was 7:30 am. 'The broadcast by Delphine Felix, the Prime Minister, will commence in 30 seconds, 29 seconds, 28 seconds....'

'I wonder how many others are watching?' Clare asked.

'24 seconds...'

'Anyone who was asked to, I expect. None of us can

afford to lose our pensions love.'

'19 seconds…'

'But, why us?' she said picking at the raw skin on the side of her thumb.

Martin shrugged.

'10 seconds.'

'Maybe we're about to find out,' he said kissing her swiftly on her cheek.

'4 seconds, 3, 2, 1.'

The clock faded, replaced by pulses of green, blue, purple and red. An outline of something moved within each colour, as if it were trying to push its way out from behind the screen. Then the sound of a heart beating, like on a terrible reality show. A bemused, nervous smile spread across their faces.

'Concentrate Mr and Mrs Carter, show some respect,' a voice from the tablet said. Martin and Clare straightened, eyes forward, grasping each other's hand.

As the camera pulled back, Delphine Felix's face filled the screen in vivid close up. She was a striking, angular kind of woman. Mid-thirties with poker straight bleached blonde hair, penetrating brown eyes framed under her trademark black brows. Years of girl band photo shoots had embedded some kid of muscle memory into her crimson lips which tensed, parted then micro pouted before she spoke in her breathy, from nowhere in particular accent.

'Good morning to all 20,000 of you watching across England, on this my first broadcast of the day. Our Pensioners have been an undervalued and underutilised resource. This is about to change. You, the mature citizens of this country are critical to our success as a nation going forward. You have been identified as the perfect group to become our Community Observers. You will play a crucial role in supporting the implementation of the National Order. You will be instrumental in the transition to our new society.

Your role will be to monitor a group of citizens in your neighbourhood and report any behaviour infringements. Your monitoring work will be aligned to the four pillars of the National Order: Environment, Energy, Health and Citizen Compliance. A Community Observer Co-ordinator will contact you shortly after this broadcast with further details.

So why have we selected you for this critical role? In your lifetimes you have witnessed and embraced technological changes like no other generation before you, experienced changes in our society, our culture, our behaviours, our environment and our health. Your experience is unique among us. As a resource you should not be wasted. And there are many benefits to harnessing your latent potential, not only for the country as a whole but for you as individuals. Your work as a Community Observer will keep you active and engaged. Mental and physical activity will improve your wellbeing, reducing the burden of preventable elderly care on the Health Service. Knowing that you are making a positive contribution to society will enable you to enjoy a meaningful and fulfilled later life. And of course, you will be rewarded for your contribution.

Thank you for your co-operation and your support,' she paused, looking earnestly into the camera. Delphine still knew how to work a crowd, 'I know, we can count on you.'

The tablet switched itself off. Clare's mouth fell open but no sound came out. Martin flopped back into his chair.

NICKY SMOOTHED OUT the letter, streaking it with grease and gritty crumbs from her buttery fingers. She stuffed the remainder of the second slab of toast into her empty mouth and began to read.

Ministry of Citizen Compliance
Government House
London

29 October 2029

Dear Miss Nicholls,

The final phase of the Government's Society Reform Programme, Citizen Compliance, will be implemented from January 1ˢᵗ 2030 when the National Order will become law.

All means of electronic communication will cease at midnight 31ˢᵗ December 2029. From January 1ˢᵗ 2030 communication will be by letter, telephone or in person only, for a period of time yet to be determined. Electronic communication will be restored in phases thereafter.

In preparation for these changes, you will receive an email from us on November 5ᵗʰ 2029. You will be asked to confirm your personal details, including your height and weight as recorded by your Doctor at your recent Resource Impact Assessment.

You will be asked to confirm your acceptance of the National Order. Failure to accept will require you to undertake training that will facilitate your effective participation in society as described in the Citizen Compliance charter.

Yours sincerely,

Robert Chatterjee – Jones, Minister for National Order

She tossed the letter into the bin, chewing furiously.

THE GOVERNMENT AUTO downloaded ringtone tore through the silence at number 22.

'Hello Martin, I'm Liv Khan your coordinator for all things National Order,' she said before he could speak. 'If Clare is with you can you put me on speaker, it'll save me another call.'

'You're on speaker,' they said in unison.

'Excellent, excellent, oh and voice recognition already authenticated for both of you. Isn't technology marvellous? I can tell you're both going to be perfect. Now, you're scheduled for intensive training in Harrogate from the 9th to the 19th November. It'll blow your minds, honestly, you'll love it! So, if you have any plans, cancel them, simple as that. And no need to worry about your cat, it'll be placed in a veterinary facility while you're away – call it a first perk of the job. I'll send you full details of all the arrangements. But it's important to say upon successful completion of your training, your pension will increase by 37.7 %. You will receive bonus payments based on your performance in the job, but we'll go into all of that at training. Unfortunately, if you don't pass, your pension will be reduced by 42.5%, so that's an incentive to do your best if ever there was one! And I must stress, for your own security,' Liv paused as she had been instructed at this point, 'you must not discuss any aspect of the broadcast this morning or this conversation with anyone. See you on the 9th.'

She hung up.

Martin turned to his wife and wiped the tear from her cheek.

'And to think we voted for Delphine Felix. What she promised, how she said it would be....it's not this,' he whispered.

'Well it is when you really think about it. It's not the what that's wrong, it's the how. We were all just too lazy or ignorant or trusting to ask about the how, ask for the details.' Clare stood up, cradling the cat like a baby, 'I'll put the kettle on.'

'What were we thinking love?' he asked.

'We weren't thinking Martin, that's the problem, we never do. We should have learned by now.'

NICKY WAS IN bed, her laptop next to her. On the bedside table a cup of warm milk and whisky nestled among an assortment of snack detritus. The hot water bottle, balanced on her bloated menstrual abdomen, slid off as she jabbed at the flapjack crumbs scattered across the duvet with her moistened finger.

'Audrey, open my email,' she said to her laptop. The first was from the Ministry of Compliance. Her eyes widened, 'Jesus, here we go,' she said.

Subject: Citizen Confirmation

5 November 2029

Please check your personal information. Report any errors by return.

Click on the circle to confirm your details are correct.

Click on the hexagon to confirm you accept the terms and conditions of the National Order. <u>Failure to click the box will require you to undertake appropriate training.</u>

Thank you for your anticipated cooperation as a compliant citizen.

Your Resource Impact Risk rating: HIGH

Your Personal Information:

Name: Miss Nicola Jane Nicholls
Address: 14 Highland Road, Oldwood, Yorkshire
            OW14 4DG
D.o.B: 16 May 2004
Height: 1.54 m
Weight: 68kg   G.P supplied corrective dietary
            advice
Smoker: Yes   G.P advised ban effective 1.1.30
Citizen ref: OW16200414

'Audrey, click on the circle. Audrey, send reply.'

Nicky plunged her finger into her mouth and licked it clean.

'Audrey, shut down and lights out.'

14 Highland
Road Oldwood

November 6th 2029

Hey Susie,

This is the first letter I've EVER written! I'm not sure I've done it right. Bought a stamp — £3.10! First class! I thought I'd better give it a go before they pull the plug! I did my email confirmation thing last night. I didn't click the blue hexagon.... who do they think they are? They'll never get away with this — WankerS!!!!!!

I'm really excited about Christmas this year — we'll have a great time. I'm gonna stuff my face, (cheeky buggers say I'm a potential unfair drain on National Health resources. I'm a high risk!) and smoke my head off before the ban! Hope you won't mind me polluting your balcony even more than usual!!!! I might have got through all my packs by Christmas though ☹...sniff. The shops here are already rationing fags, I can't believe it! God knows how I'll nicotine medicate then? You couldn't pick up some for me could you? Just in case?

Anyway, I'll be with you on the 21st December, but I'll confirm again nearer the time.

Let me know when you get this letter.

Love ya lots! Nicky xxx.

Sender: Susan DuPont

Subject: Letter

November 08 2029

Hi Nicky!

Amazingly the piece of paper covered in your awful handwriting arrived! Still quite the rebel aren't you? I'm not so brave though…don't hate me. ☺

See you Dec 21st anytime after 6pm. Get your train booked **NOW!**

Lots of love,

Sooze xxx

Martin and Clare stood on the pavement outside number 22, clutching the matching grey suitcases that had been delivered the day before. It was 5.15 am on November 9th. Soft white snowflakes began to drift slowly down, settling on the frozen pavement around their feet. A short stocky figure rounded the corner, lurching from one side of the pavement to the other.

'Hey! You two off on your holidays?'

'Something like that Nicky,' Clare said.

'I'm just getting home…out last night. Passed out on a mate's floor. I'm old enough to know better, but there you go. Got to have all the fun you can get these days, right?' Nicky said waving an empty whisky bottle in front of her face. 'Here's your taxi coming by the looks and if you don't mind me saying, a bit of sun will do you both some good.' She staggered off patting her coat pockets, searching for her door keys. A navy-blue minibus with the sheen of a thoroughbred racehorse, stopped in front of them. The door slid open and Martin and Clare stepped inside.

Nobody noticed them return, or the different hours that the Carters were keeping. Their training had been intense and thorough. It was snowing hard again the morning Martin and Clare picked Nicky up at the bus stop.

'Thanks! what a pair of life savers you two are! It's freezing! We might get sent home early if this weather carries on, bloody hope so. I'm not taking you out of your way, am I?'

'You're not Nicky.' Martin said, 'buckle up.'

'I didn't recognise you at first,' she said pulling the seatbelt across her chest, 'new car?'

'New to us.' Clare replied.

'It's very….kind of, secure looking? These seatbelts are pretty, what's the word? Sturdy?'

NICKY PICKED UP the fountain pen she had been given and wrote her second ever letter.

Citizen Training Centres
Platform Alpha 3
North Sea

20th December 2029

Dear Susan,

I will be unable to visit this Christmas after all. I am sorry for the short notice and for any inconvenience that this will cause you. Please accept my sincerest apologies.

I am at a Government Training Centre to complete my Citizenship Training and Rehabilitation Programme in order to comply with the Citizen Compliance Charter.

I will be returning to a community as an Ambassador for the Government's Society Reform Programme, not to Oldwood though. I may not be able to be in touch again for some time but I will as soon as I can.

With very best wishes for the Festive Season,
Nicola.

Trainee Citizen A1398

The bald man with the booming voice stood up. 'Congratulations all. Day one in the classroom is complete. The real work begins tomorrow. Go back to your cabins and get ready for dinner. Leave your letters on your desk. They'll go to the mainland tonight.'

Nicky folded her letter in half, the only act of defiance her dulled brain could manage, then filtered into line with the others.

MARTIN AND CLARE sat on their new sofa. The cat lay in between them on his new sheepskin blanket with his name, Trevor, embroidered across the corner.

'More wine love?' Clare asked.

'Of course,' Martin smiled, 'we've more than earned it.'

'We have. Top performers, quarter one. Well done us! I never thought we'd take to the work. This life,' Clare said wistfully pouring the wine, 'but after Nicky, getting the first one out of the way, that was the turning point wasn't it? For me anyway. It's kind of easy now isn't it? And we're a good team.'

'It's the money,' Martin said taking a long slow drink of the Merlot. 'That first bonus payment, that was the turning point for me! I mean it was our best Christmas in a long time. And we can have the heating on all day, all night if we want. Life is good. Delphine promised it would be.'

'Not just for us though. We are doing some good. We

are making a difference and people like Nicky, people like that, they will thank us, eventually. I know they will. I wonder where she is now?'

'Not for us to know, or bother ourselves about.'

'The couple who've moved into her place look nice enough,' Clare said. 'I'll call in on them tomorrow, try get us an invite to spend some time around there.'

Two hundred miles away a clean-cut young man smiled.

'Compliance check complete' he said. The microphone inserted under Trevor's skin was transmitting perfectly.

Ticket

Sherri Turner

I AM WAITING in this plastic place that doesn't smell of hope when it should, when I need it to, and the machine in the corner is clicking down numbers like seconds left, only much more slowly and my number is still a long way off, number eighty-two and the counter is on seventeen and I look around and there are only four people waiting so how can that be right and I go to the desk and say I think you've given me the wrong ticket and the woman looks up at me through her glasses, and says blue ticket machine and points with her pen without stopping writing and I see it in the corner and take another ticket and it says twenty-two which is better, or worse, not so long to wait and the numbers on the machine flip over twenty-one, twenty-two and it is my turn and the doctor half-looks at me kindly and speaks slowly so that I can understand only I don't really and all I can think is that they've given me the wrong ticket again but they haven't.

The Pendulum

James Northern

REBECCA FEARED THE worst as she pushed open the front door; she hadn't had tenants here for months and hadn't come in as often as she'd planned, despite only living across the road. But as she went from room to room, she found no dust on the windowsills or on the light mahogany furniture, nor any damp on the cream-coloured walls. The coal in the fireplace was covered in white specks, which was odd as she could swear that she'd replaced it when the previous tenants left. There were plates and mugs in the drying rack in the kitchen, but no sign of forced entry through any of the doors or windows. It must have been the real estate agents, but why would they, or anyone else for that matter, be eating and drinking in her house? It was when she was outside on the veranda, closing up the property, that she thought she heard whispering. She stopped and listened for a moment. Perhaps it was her imagination or the crisp golden leaves blowing across the decking.

She descended the wooden steps onto the sidewalk and began to cross the road when she heard three loud knocks behind her. When she turned around, the tall figure of a man was standing at the lounge window of the house from which she'd come. He was staring straight at her, his brow knotted and his lips drawn tight. The sun lit his wrinkled face and reflected off the thin layer of silver hair on his head. It was as if he'd been there all these years and she'd simply stopped visiting him; it used to be his house after all, before she'd inherited it.

'YOU SURE IT was your Grandpa?' asked Barbara, leaning across the table in the cafe while cradling her mug in her hands. Her coffee was as black as her hair and just a shade or two darker than the bags that hung beneath her eyes.

'Of course I am,' said Rebecca. 'I'd know that gaze anywhere. Nobody could disapprove like he could.'

'So, what did you do?'

'I got startled. A car honked its horn right next to me. I'd been standing in the middle of the road and hadn't seen it coming. And then, when I looked back at the house, he'd gone.'

'Did you go back?' asked Barbara.

'No point. I'd entered every room. Opened every cupboard. Anyway, he died nearly two years ago, so he can't really have been there.'

'I think I remember him. He didn't like Tony much, did he?'

'He didn't like most things,' said Rebecca. She looked at her watch before scooping up her museum leaflets from the table and tucking them into her purple leather handbag. 'I'd better get going. My babysitter finishes in an hour.'

Soon, they were walking along the National Mall beside the long expanse of grass that stretched between the shining white dome of the Capitol building and the giant obelisk-shaped Washington monument. As they drew near to the square base of the monument, they found themselves approaching a large crowd, which was flowing steadily in the direction of the White House. Chanting filled the air and hundreds of cardboard placards, all of them still a little too distant to be read, swayed above the mob.

'Of course, the protests!' said Barbara. 'I totally forgot.'

They doubled back, making for a different Metro station, but they'd barely moved a block from the Mall when they encountered a navy blue army of pale-skinned men with helmets and plastic shields.

'Let's try a different stop,' said Rebecca.

'No,' replied Barbara, 'we can still get through here.'

'You know, I don't know how you can still work for him.'

'Who?'

'The President.'

'I hardly work for him, Becca. I'm not a politician; I'm a federal employee, and I'm not exactly senior.'

'But you enact his policies.'

'I enact the policies that people voted for.'

'But the evictions—'

'They're what people wanted. Anyway, I thought we weren't going to talk about this anymore.'

Rebecca sighed. The chorus of chants was more distant now, but also louder, if anything, and punctuated by sharp intermittent yells. 'Same time next week?' she asked, eager to descend below ground and leave town.

'Absolutely!'

They exchanged a stiff hug.

'You're lucky,' said Barbara. 'Wish I had a baby to go home to.'

THE BABYSITTER WAS young—too young, Rebecca had thought at first—with flowing auburn hair that reached so far down her back that it might have counted as a limb. But Carol, as she was called, had proven to have a gentle manner and a soothing effect on little Jack, for whom she seemed to have genuine affection. She pulled open the front door with long delicate arms and smiled at Rebecca as if seeing a member of her own family.

Rebecca grimaced in return. 'Sorry I'm late,' she said.

'I'm just glad you made it out of DC,' said Carol. 'Was it bad?'

'Just getting started when I left.'

'He's been on edge today.'

'I hope he's not been difficult.'

'Maybe he can sense the storm.'

'Of course, there's a storm coming in this evening, isn't there? Guess I'll leave Wegmans till the morning.'

Rebecca paid Carol and went to lift Jack out of the turquoise playpen in the living room.

She sat on the couch and positioned him on her lap. He immediately clawed at her breast, but before she fed him, she managed to snatch the TV remote in her left hand, pass it over to her right and press several buttons with her thumb. It was a well-practised manoeuvre. A news channel lit the television set, the only news channel still broadcasting.

'This just in: ugly scenes in the nation's capital where crowds have gathered to protest against immigration laws passed by Presidential decree in the summer. Our correspondent, Roger McMillan, is here to tell us more.'

REBECCA STRUGGLED TO sleep that night. The winds howled around the wooden frame of the building as raindrops battered the windows and water streamed into the gutter. She had notched up the heating before going to bed. At least Jack was sleeping quietly. She picked up her cell phone from her bedside table and thought for a moment: it was late, but he probably wouldn't mind. She opened the contacts and selected Tony. It rang twice before he picked up.

'Rebecca.' But the voice wasn't Tony's. 'Hello?'

'Rebecca.'

'Grandpa?'

She hung up.

She was on her feet now, pulling back the curtains from the bedroom window and looking through the gloom toward the empty property across the road. She could just make it out through the misty rain and the water running over the glass. It was the spitting image of the house she inhabited with its horizontal white panelling on the outside walls, its columned veranda and an upstairs bedroom protruding from its steep black roof. But when she squinted through the glare of the street lamps, she noticed something unusual. A faint orange light glimmered behind the closed living room curtains, and smoke appeared to be rising from the chimney to meet the dark, drifting clouds. There was somebody inside.

She thought about calling for help, but what if this was another inexplicable apparition and there was nothing to see when the cops turned up? She didn't fancy a stint in the funny farm; Jack had lost one parent already. Besides, if her Grandpa had returned in some way and in some form, shouldn't she at least try to speak to him? They'd not got on ever since she'd met Tony, but she regretted the state of their relationship when he died. Yes, he'd become increasingly bitter and malevolent in his old age, bigoted even, but he was still family, and she knew that, on some level, he'd always cared for her. He'd left her his house after all. True, her mother's accident hadn't left him many options, but he could have found something else to do with it. She looked in on Jack in the room next to hers: he was still fast asleep in his cot, his little chest rising and falling in rhythm. He'd be fine. She'd only be out a couple minutes.

Wearing her raincoat over her pyjamas, its hood pulled over her straggled blonde hair, Rebecca sprinted across the road and mounted the wooden steps onto the veranda of her Grandpa's old house. Her slippers were sodden by the time she arrived and squelched with every step. She nearly slipped on a patch of wet leaves before steadying herself on the handle of the front door and fumbling the keys into the lock.

A wave of warm air washed over her as she stepped inside. 'Hello!' she called out. The house was quiet but alive with shadows that flickered in the light emanating from the lounge. The lounge door was ajar and creaked as she pushed it open. She'd never noticed it creak before now. Inside, the room was empty, but the fireplace held strong crackling flames behind its protective golden grate. There was a depression in one of the black leather armchairs, as if somebody had been sitting there moments earlier.

'Hello!' she called again. She ran her fingers over the dip, feeling the angle, assuring herself that it was real.

Thinking suddenly of Jack, she went over to the window to look back across at the house in which she lived, but as she drew back the curtains, she felt a presence behind her, a slight shift in the atmosphere.

'Who's there?' she asked, freezing with her hand on the curtain. She heard the creak of the door and a squeak from the floorboards. Somebody was in the room. She turned around.

A heavily-built African American man stood before her in a black T-shirt and blue jeans. Behind him were two men that looked like Latinos. What a dumb idea it had been to come over here on her own.

'You live here?' asked the African American.

'Across the road,' said Rebecca, trying to sound more confident than she felt. 'I own this place. Who are you?'

'Laru.'

'Is that your name?'

He nodded in a way that made her feel ignorant.

'Can we stay a night?' he asked.

Rebecca allowed the words to sink in. 'You want to

stay in my house?'

He nodded patiently.

'You're illegals, aren't you?' she asked.

The Latinos exchanged a glance.

'We'll leave soon,' said Laru.

'To where?'

'Canada.'

'Ah, Canada. I get it. Everybody's going there.' She raised her hands a little and let them slap against her thighs. 'Well, OK then. I guess you can stay a night or two. Just keep out of sight, and don't get too comfortable.'

'You won't tell anyone?'

'Like…'

'Like the authorities.'

'I don't much like the authorities.' She surprised herself with the venom in her voice.

'Stay a couple days. I've got nobody moving in.'

One of the Latinos threw a look out of the open lounge door into the hallway. Rebecca heard a metallic click and the fumble of clothing before another man entered the room. He had white skin, tattoos on his neck and a shaven head.

'And where are *you* from?' she asked.

'Fairfax, Virginia.' he replied.

'That's Mason. He's Jewish,' said Laru.

'Since when have Jewish people needed to flee America?' asked Rebecca.

'I know the history of my people,' replied Mason, taking a seat on the settee.

'He's our fixer,' said Laru.

'YOU BROUGHT THEM provisions?' asked Barbara, her mouth remaining open a little longer than was necessary. She'd shaken a few drops of coffee over the rim of her mug and onto her fingers. She and Rebecca were sitting opposite each other in a service station just off the interstate; downtown Washington was no longer safe. Rebecca stirred her hot chocolate, carving dark swirls of brown into its milky foam. She glanced to either side of her: they were still alone in a deserted corner of the cafe.

'I got them a few things at Wegmans. Not much; just enough. Why not?'

'They're illegals aren't they? Surely that's ... well, illegal?' said Barbara.

'They're only illegal since the administration decided they were illegal, which was, like, two months ago.'

'Four months ago. And do you have any idea what they would do to me at work if they find out I've suppressed this?'

'Oh, come on, Barbara. We've been friends since kindergarten. If I can't talk to you, who can I talk to? They're only going to be here another couple days. One of them was a teacher in Baltimore, and another was a chef in a diner.'

They sat in silence, sipping at the remainder of their drinks. Rebecca's cell phone buzzed. She picked it up off the table and looked at the screen: the first live round had been fired at the protesters. She was about to tell Barbara when she noticed her friend's appearance, the patches around her eyes that were growing darker by the day, the gaunt look of sleeplessness. Had she lost weight too?

'How have *you* been doing, anyway?' Rebecca asked, softening her voice.

'Oh, you know how it is,' said Barbara. 'Cuts in federal funding. Applying for my own job. Two people, one job. My hometown is a war zone. You seen your ghost again lately? I probably look like him.'

'You have to apply for your own job?'

'Against a colleague and a friend. Well, a former friend now. I guess I just have to...' she made a sharp jabbing motion with her elbow.

Rebecca laughed.

That night, she was sitting on the couch in the living room with a cold bottle of beer in her hand—mother's prerogative. Jack was sound asleep in the cot in his room. She took a sip from her bottle and rolled the bitterness around in her mouth. The television was broadcasting the news channel: more evictions taking place despite the protests, the politicians unanimous in their support. Well, they would be wouldn't they, the ones who were still politicians?

How had her country come to this? Only a few years beforehand, it had felt like an increasingly liberal and progressive democracy. Rebecca had studied law and politics at college and knew all about the toing and froing of ideology in the history of human ideas, the way that each prevailing philosophy had always been replaced, in turn, by its opposite, like the swinging of a giant pendulum. But usually, over time, gradual progress was made and society inched its way forward. This felt different. Things had gotten extreme. It was as if the pendulum had swung too far. She'd emigrate if she could, but her little family needed her; she was its only breadwinner and couldn't take risks with her income. Jobs were hard to come by everywhere these days, even for Harvard-educated lawyers like her.

Three knocks sounded on the front door, not too loud but distinct. Rebecca placed her beer on the coffee table and padded through the hallway in her slippers. That's strange: nobody was about. She returned to the living room.

'This is the greatest social reform agenda any government has ever undertaken,' a White House spokesman was saying.

Three knocks again. Kids? At this time?

She went back to the door, this time opening it and

calling out to anybody that might be lurking in the night-time shadows. The streetlamp near her house was flickering, but there was no other sign of movement, not even a fox. When she returned to the living room, the air felt cold. Her breath was visible as a small white cloud when she exhaled, but she'd only held the door open for a few seconds and the central heating was on. Was it her imagination or had the light got dimmer too? No, it wasn't the light: the TV was switched off. She didn't remember doing that. She picked up the remote and was about to press a button, when a low hiss arose all around her, as if it were emanating from the walls, the floor and the ceiling all at once. It grew in volume until it formed into a whisper, words, her name, repeated over and over, 'Rebecca, Rebecca.'

'The hell with you!' she yelled. 'Why don't you just show yourself and speak to me! What do you want anyway?'

A silence fell on the room, which was punctured by a faint murmuring from upstairs; she'd woken Jack. Next came short regular creaks of straining wood, the pitch slightly changing each time, as if it were becoming more distant, but she couldn't quite place it. What was going on? Where was he? What was he doing? Then she understood. She arrived at the bottom of the stairs in time to see something disappear from the top step. She glimpsed a shadow passing along an upstairs wall. The volume at which Jack could wail, even at six months of age, had never ceased to amaze her, but she'd never heard such terror in his cry as she did just then.

In five or six giant steps, she mounted the staircase and launched open the door to his bedroom. Once inside, she had eyes for one thing alone. Jack had levered himself to his feet and was standing against the side of his cot, gripping the vertical wooden bars. His eyes were tightly shut and his mouth fully open as he called out for help. Rebecca slipped her hands under his arms, lifted him to her chest and bounded back down the staircase. She managed to grab her keys on the way to the front door and, once outside, made straight for the car. She secured Jack into his baby seat in the back, clambered into the driver's seat, slamming the door shut behind her, and twisted the keys in the ignition. She saw no pursuer as she reversed away. She'd left the door unlocked, but it wasn't the time to worry about that.

'It's alright Jack, we're safe now,' she repeated, over and over, as her baby calmed himself in the back of the vehicle. If only she could calm herself as easily. She joined the interstate heading north and began to feel some relief as the signposts flicked past and woodland area drifted by the windows like dark clouds. A service station approached and she contemplated stopping to buy coffee; the adrenaline was leaving her blood and tiredness was beginning to take over. Jack was asleep now. She turned on the car radio—that would keep her awake, surely.

'… seen crowds like this afternoon. This was civil disorder on an unprecedented scale…'

The voice faded out. Rebecca tapped at the buttons on the radio, but she was unable to find any station that returned anything but static. She gave up and turned it off. The road was almost empty, and the car was eating up the miles, but it would take her hours to reach her destination. Maybe she couldn't emigrate herself, but she could at least deliver Jack to safety, because whether she was hallucinating or being haunted, one thing was for sure: he wasn't safe with her right now.

She noticed her surroundings brighten and realised that it must be the headlamps from an approaching car behind her. She glanced into the rear-view mirror, but the light dimmed again; something in front of her back window seemed to be obscuring her view. She turned on the interior lights of the vehicle and looked again into the mirror.

He was sitting next to Jack in the backseat of her car with his wide, vacant eyes, and his ever-present white shirt. He looked as real as anything else, his white hair reflecting orange whenever a streetlamp passed by. Rebecca hit the brake, bringing them to a halt in the hard shoulder. Soon, she was standing at the roadside and bouncing Jack gently in her arms. There was no sign of the old man; he'd gone as suddenly as he'd appeared.

Another car had stopped behind her. It had a dark colour and a yellow stripe printed along the side above the words 'Maryland Transit Police.' A cop strode over. He was a pale, overweight man with strands of greasy brown hair protruding from beneath his cap.

'You trying to kill us both, lady?' he said. 'I'm really sorry. I think I'm just... tired.'

'What's your name?'

'Rebecca.'

'Rebecca ...'

'O'Grady.'

'Whereabouts you heading, Rebecca O'Grady?'

'Canada.'

'Canada? At this time of night? It's Sunday tomorrow. Maybe you should stop over until the morning? There's a motel back there at the services.'

The man had a point. Besides, she and Jack were obviously no safer on the road than they were anywhere else. Probably less safe, in fact. She was going to have to find another solution. Maybe she'd spend the night with her new neighbours across the road. Safety in numbers. The cop was staring at her baby with a smile playing on his lips.

'He's called Jack,' she said.

'He's cute,' said the cop. 'Looks a little Latino, if you ask me.'

'Everybody says that,' she replied, laughing.

SUNDAY AFTERNOON WAS warm and the queues to
Starbucks poured out of the door and along the street.
Rebecca and Barbara ordered take-out coffee and carried
their steaming white cups along the seafront. The sky was
clear and a gentle breeze was blowing. Jack was straining
against the straps in his stroller as he waved his arms at the
white boats in the Marina, which tilted back and forth as
if dancing for his pleasure.

'You've still not seen a physician, have you?' asked
Barbara.

'And you still think I'm crazy.'

'I didn't say that, Becca, but you're clearly having
hallucinations. There's no stigma to it these days.'

'Then how come it's not just me who can see him?
Jack screamed when he entered his room.'

Barbara thought for a moment. 'You could have hal-
lucinated the scream,' she pointed out. 'People have
auditory hallucinations. Or you might have scared Jack
when you yelled. Babies often pick up on a mother's
emotions. I'm just saying at least consider the possibility
that you might have something like ... I don't know,
like—'

'—like paranoid schizophrenia?'

'Right.'

'I don't. I looked it up. The symptoms are wrong.
Anyway, that's the thing, isn't it? We're all a little
paranoid these days, all looking over our shoulders,

watching our backs, blaming strangers for whatever is wrong in our lives.'

Barbara rolled her eyes.

'What happened about your job, anyway?' asked Rebecca, 'I've been worried about you.'

'Vacancy doesn't close for another week. I *have* to get it, Becca, or I'm in trouble. You're lucky with your law firm. You never have to worry about money. I think I have a plan now, but I'd have to upset somebody, and I hate doing that.'

'Well, you can't always please everybody, can you?'

'Very true, Becca. I know, I have too much empathy sometimes. It's annoying.'

REBECCA HADN'T SLEPT all night. It was the early hours of the morning and she'd been lying in bed for hours, aware of every rustle and bump, every animal cry that was carried through the suburban streets where she lived. She'd been waiting to hear three knocks on the front door, just like the previous evening. She even thought that she'd heard them once but wasn't sure enough to move and had waited with bated breath for a repeat that never came. When the knocks did come, there was no mistaking them, a set of three again, loud and crisp, echoing up the stairs and across the landing into her room. This time, she managed not to panic—funny how exhaustion could make her brave. Instead, she took the time to pull on her slippers and wrap her body in a light purple dressing gown before making her way downstairs. There were another three knocks before she reached the ground floor, followed by shouting. It didn't sound much like an old man. When she opened the front door, she found three uniformed officers with 'Police' and 'ICE' emblazoned in white lettering on their uniforms. They were all men and all six foot or so in height with white skin and muscular frames.

'Could you step outside a second, Ma'am?' one of the officers said, 'I need to ask you some questions.'

She took a careful step out onto the wooden flooring of the veranda. The sun had not yet begun to rise and she felt a sharp chill in the air, but in truth, she'd begun to tremble long before she'd left the warmth of her hallway.

'Could you give me your name, please?' the officer asked. His two clones stood behind him, so Rebecca reasoned that he must be in charge.

'Rebecca O'Grady,' she said.

'O'Grady is your maiden name, right?'

'No.'

'Your married name is Ricci.'

'Actually, no. I changed it back a few months ago.'

'You changed it back?'

'Uh-huh.'

'One moment please.'

The officer walked down the steps onto her drive and exchanged some words with the occupant of an unmarked grey car, whom Rebecca couldn't quite make out. She looked across the road and saw two more cars parked at her other property, the house that was supposed to be empty. The door was open, the lights were on in several of the rooms and dark shadows could be seen in motion behind the curtains. She averted her eyes, trying to feign disinterest.

The lead officer returned to her front door. 'Does Antonio Ricci live here?' he asked.

'Not anymore.'

'Where is he now?'

'Tony moved to Canada.'

'Canada?'

'That's what I said.'

'And Giacomo Ricci.'

'Jack is just a baby!'

'Does he live here, Ma'am?'

She took a deep breath. 'No.'

'Where—'

'Canada.'

The officer turned to the two men behind him and nodded his head. They sprang into motion and pushed past Rebecca into her house. He remained outside and began to pace up and down her veranda, talking into his radio. A single thought occurred to her in an instant:

Barbara. Could she even be there now, at the scene? Rebecca waited until the officer was pacing away from her and then seized the opportunity to stride, unopposed, down the wooden steps that led to the car on her drive. Crouching down, she peered through the windows, seeing one white female officer, but no sign of Barbara.

'Would you come back up here please, Ma'am? I don't want to have to take you in.' Rebecca did as she was told. The man was polite, she'd give him that.

Five minutes later, several ICE officers arrived from across the road and reported that the house opposite was empty. Then the two emerged from Rebecca's front door.

'Nobody here,' one of them said. The lead officer looked at Rebecca for a moment as if he expected her to explain. Soon, they were leaving, the glowing lights on their dark vehicles crawling in slow procession along the road. The sky was just starting to brighten, the blackness registering its first shade of blue.

Rebecca looked across the road to her Grandpa's old house. The front door swung on its hinges. She remembered arriving there the previous evening with a small, warm bundle in her arms, gripping it tightly while trying to hold herself together. Mason had answered the door and let her in. 'He's not safe here anymore,' she'd said to Laru as she placed Jack into his arms. Laru had stared at the baby with the same expression he'd worn when he'd first seen Rebecca on the day that she'd found him in her property. 'Please do this for me,' said Rebecca. 'Take him to Toronto and, when you get there, look for a guy called Antonio Ricci. He's in the Italian quarter. I can give you his number.'

Laru thought for a moment and then nodded. 'We're ready to leave,' he said.

A few hours later, at just gone midnight, four men and a baby had entered the back of a nondescript white van that had stopped to pick them up. Rebecca kept a tight grip on herself until the van was out of sight, and then the tears began to flow. Now, in the slowly brightening morning, she looked at the road along which her son had departed a few hours beforehand.

Some of the neighbours were watching her through the upstairs windows protruding from their rooftops. They'd probably seen her whole encounter with the law. And there, in the middle of the road, stood her Grandpa with a look of cold satisfaction his face. Rebecca returned his stare; she was no longer afraid of him. What was the worst he could do to her now? If he was here with her, he wasn't with Jack. That was the gamble she'd taken. Whether he was a ghost or something out of her own subconscious—a symbol perhaps, or a warning—at least she now thought that she understood why he'd returned. The country was right for him now. He fitted in. The fear of ghosts, Rebecca realised, was not just the fear of the unknown, but the fear of the past recurring. She was sure of another thing too: in time, her family would return. They'd be together again, the three of them, in this place. The pendulum would swing again—it had to, it was the way of things—and when it did, it must never be allowed to come here again.

She strode back inside, leaving the door to click shut on the chilly morning air.

The President Comes Home

Reshma Ruia

THE PRESIDENT'S HEART is failing. He has spent months nurturing this pain.

'But there are orders to be signed and laws to be passed.'

The Ministers point to the dusty files on his ivory desk. The President shakes his head, hands rubbing his chest.

'There is a wound here that won't heal,' he says.

The Ministers fear a coup. Telephone calls are made. Faxes sent in the hush of night. A fleet of silver-haired doctors fly in from Switzerland, armed with stethoscopes and sugar coated pills.

They poke and prod but can't find the root.

'No tumour, no abscess, no perforated lung or limb,' they say, as they tot up their bill.

The President offers them rooibos tea, cardamom macaroons and platters of plantain chips.

At daybreak, he has them lined outside the palace

walls and dispatched to heaven with a single gunshot.

The pain persists. A lover's kiss, it feeds on his skin. One night a young man appears in his dream. He says:

Go back to your village and become one with your people. The President knows him. It's Jesus, showing him the way.

THE PRESIDENT'S ROLLS Royce glides towards his ancestral village, past ochre anthills and bare fields shaved of crop. Goose feather pillows cushion his back, a rosary of pearls dangles from his wrist. One fat index finger rests on a page of King James' Bible. His eyes, sunk within their folds of fat weep.

In the village, the men rush to button their rags. The women sweep their huts clean. Empty-bellied dogs, the old and the sick are pushed out of sight and told to hide the ditch. The villagers wait with folded hands and toes curled in fright.

The President steps out of his bullet proof Rolls Royce. His chauffeur spreads a velvet rug beneath his feet. The President kicks it aside. He kneels down, forehead pressed to the ground. When he raises his head, his cheeks are smeared with grey brown dust that looks like ash.

'Help me rise,' he shouts to his aide de camp. With a huff and a puff, he's pulled to his feet.

Slowly he strips, discarding his Saville Row suiting.

The pinstriped jacket with the scarlet lining goes first. There's a gasp and a lone titter as he unbuckles his belt. The sun makes the buckle glint like gold. His shoes handmade in Italy and his father's ruby ring join the pile. Naked he stands before his people, hands cupped like a begging bowl.

'I have come to mend my heart. To be one with you. It's what Jesus wants, he says in his best Queen's English voice.

The villagers scratch their heads and scream, 'We want our President back with his diamonds and his guns.' They gather their sticks and shoo him away.

The President runs trips and falls. His heart leaps out through a crack.

'Aaaahh,' the President sighs, holding his heart in his fist like a rose.

Peace. At last!

Prime Meridian

Geoffrey Graves

IT WAS THE first day of spring, the vernal equinox, and it was raining cats and dogs. Not water droplets. Inexplicably, worldwide, real cats and dogs were floating down like dry leaves from the skies. The dogs: Cairn Terriers, Dachshunds, Basset Hounds, Poodles, Dalmatians, Sharpeis and Great Danes. The cats: Siamese, Persian, Abyssinian, Sphynx, Bengal, Exotic Short-Haired.

Cats!

Dogs!

Their impact with the pavement, roofs, trees and car tops didn't harm the animals because at the last minute of descent their descents slowed to a gentle soft landing. Every cat wafted airily down on its cushioning paw pads, somehow managing to circumvolve with that last second instinctual twirl cats have that allows for a simultaneous quad-paw landing. The dogs, to their credit unembarrassed to be stealing the patented kitty-cat move, slowly rotated in a similar, delicate, tabby-like touchdown. Some didn't come all the way down and were left drifting inches off the ground for a good ten minutes till they, too, connected with terra firma. It was fun to watch.

That night TV weather reporters showed videos of felines and canines scudding out of the clouds. The highlight was the Great Dane that eased down atop the head of an unsuspecting Tokyo newsman during a live report while holding a recently descended Turkish Angora kitten. The curious awaited the experts' explanations but they had none, their degrees from Weather U useless. Those meteorologists never got the weather right anyway, thought the populace, why should we expect anything different now?

Kids loved it and ran out into the streets to scoop up as many of the animals as their arms would hold, carrying the arrivals into homes where they begged parents to let them keep the foundling critters. CEO'S of pet food manufacturers were on the phone to staff, demanding the immediate ramping up of production; so many new mouths to feed, so much more pet food to sell! For the next few weeks veterinarians were overwhelmed neutering, spading and administering vaccines. Happily, every single cat and dog fallen from the heavens was adopted.

These sky creatures, as people were calling them, could do everything any Earth cat or dog could do, but they did one thing more. Like Dr. Doolittle's animals, they spoke, and had a message for anyone with ears to hear. It was: 'Get with the program.' That was all they said and they said it frequently, antagonizing humans to the point of exasperation. If you asked if they needed to go out to do their business, they would answer, 'Get with the program.' Are you hungry? Want your kibble, Sparky? 'Get with the program.' Are you ready for nighty-night, Cuddles? 'Get with the program.'

The entire world was flummoxed. It didn't take long to understand there was no reason to speak to these canines and felines. Everyone knew what the answer would be.

An Australian veterinarian who was preparing to administer a distemper shot to one of the sky dogs, a Basset Hound named Spoolie, had an idea. He put his finger under the dog's chin, raising its head so they were eye-to-eye, and he said to the dog, 'What program?' The hound broke eye contact, looked away to shake his head vigorously, his long hound dog ears and loose flews flapping with every shake. Then the canine stopped. The vet took the dog's snout in hand, moved his head back so they were again dog eyeball to man eyeball, and the vet persisted: 'What program?' he demanded emphatically as though he were giving the Basset Hound a stern command to sit.

Spoolie didn't move and remained staring at the vet with an undoglike intense gaze. The vet looked over at his lanky young assistant with an oversized Adams apple that had one hair sprouting from it. The assistant, standing on the opposing side of the examination table, looked from dog to vet and back to dog. He'd had enough. He put his hands on his hips, bent down, swallowed hard causing his Adams apple to bob a visible hula, and said in a loud, demanding, piccolo-high voice, 'You will tell him now what program you're talking about you, you, you exasperating mongrel!' The assistant looked up at the vet and gave a nod as much to say, there, that ought to do it, and in a way it did.

Spoolie snorted loudly ejecting dog snot into the vet's hand and said, 'I don't know, but you'd better figure it out quickly.'

Baffled, the vet again looked at his assistant who was as puzzled as the vet. 'F-f- figure what out quickly?' the vet stammered.

The hound scratched aggressively behind his ear and said, 'I don't know, but you'd better figure it out quickly.'

'Yes, I heard you say that,' reasoned the vet, 'but what is it I am supposed to figure out quickly?'

'I don't know, but you'd better figure it out quickly,' repeated Spoolie.

Word of the vet/Spoolie encounter spread like kudzu through Georgia via social media, and indeed all sky creatures around the world had now switched to Spoolie's inculcated new phrase whenever anyone asked them, 'What program?' The scene played out in homes and veterinary hospitals; on street corners of Bangladesh; in back yards of Shanghai; and city parks of Antananarivo, Madagascar. Everyone was asking every sky dog and cat, 'What is it I am supposed to figure out quickly?' eliciting the same response in whatever the local language. Regular earth-bound dogs and cats were oblivious to the situation.

No one liked being told they had better figure out something quickly though there was no way to know what it was they'd better figure out. It was unnerving, but like many things that at first seem abnormal and bizarre, the animals' repetition of the peculiar threatening phrase eventually lost its sting. People got used to hearing the same response and the uniqueness of the situation abated. Humans stopped speaking to the sky pets because there was no use, the answer was always the same worn paradoxical sentence. Why waste your breath?

Spring turned to summer and the weather followed all its usual semi-predictable patterns leading into fall, then winter, then came spring again. Like the previous year, the vernal equinox fell on March 20, but on the day before, March 19, every sky dog and cat surprised the world once again and began saying something new. When a person neared them, they said, 'So long. Nice knowing you!' This really rattled the humans. Where were the sky animals going? Back up? To where? Was this an announcement? Was it some kind of threat? Government spy agencies and military top brass were wondering if these animals were aliens in pet clothing – a clever subterfuge of a Trojan horse invasion. 'That thing's creeping me out,' said the head of the CIA to his wife after their sky chihuahua said, 'So long. Nice knowing you!'

It was maddening! Within hours, families were lined up at animal shelters wanting to unload their sky pets. Children everywhere were crying, not wanting to give up cute little Phoebe or Fennimore. The shelters couldn't handle the volume and began turning them away. What was with these animals? They'd disrupted everything! Protests were instantly arranged with people marching in the streets holding placards that read 'Make Them Talk!' and, 'Not Nice Knowing You!' and demanding governments do something. But what? They couldn't round up all the sky creatures and put them in some massive facility, there were just too many. They couldn't exterminate them because every child on the planet with a sky animal would hate their parents forever and a day as was made clear by little Scotty Pootz when asked about it by a BBC journalist. 'Yes, I would hate me mummy and daddy forever and a day if they were to put down me little Winston.' Scotty's sky pet was a bulldog with jowls.

'And me as well,' seconded Scotty's best friend, seven-year-old Carlene Flowerday whose grammar was better than many adults'.

At United Nations headquarters in New York City,

representatives of every country met in an all night emergency session. With massive protests taking place around the globe, the pressure was on. Finally, after long hours of rancorous deliberation, they passed a vote agreeing to do something and issued a press release to that effect. It read:

'In a unanimous vote, we are very pleased to announce that all representatives of the UN have agreed to do something.' This made the world's population feel much better so all the protesters went home and the UN delegates adjourned.

The next day was humid with temperatures in the nineties. A reporter for Truth News, a major cable network, caught up with the diminutive Secretary General and stuck a microphone in his face asking what it was the UN was going to do. Affronted she'd deigned to ask him such a question, the Secretary General peered at the reporter as though she were a boil begging to be popped. He said, 'Most assuredly we will be doing something of great greatness. Have I not said that already in so many words? Something is what we will be doing! You can count on that.'

'But, sir, what is that something?' she prodded onward. 'The public wants to know.'

'My dear, let me ask you something. What is it you would do if you were me?' 'I have given it no thought, sir. I am idea-less as to what should be done.' 'Exactly!' The

Secretary General's glasses slid down to the ball on the end of his nose and he peered down at the reporter who was even shorter than he. 'That is precisely why you are not in charge and I am!'

'But, sir, surely you can share with the whole world what your plan is?'

'My plan? You want to know my plan?' The feisty reporter nodded vigorously, accidently pushing her microphone directly into the Secretary General's mouth after which he rubbed his tongue with his cuff before continuing. 'Very well, then. Here is my plan. We will do what we important representatives of the people always do. We will hire a legion of the world's most expert consultants and pay them a bundle of money to tell us what to do. Then, we will do it!'

'But no one has ever experienced such a thing before. How can we know if your experts are capable of solving such a conundrum? What if their plan doesn't work? What then?'

'Then we will do what we always do. Blame the consultants! If you paid more attention to such things you would know that. What kind of reporter are you anyway?' With that, he spun on the heels of his Berluti Scritto leather slip-on dress shoes and headed for the nearest Winchell's Donut shop for a maple iced bar and Chilla Mocha Caramel Cappuccino. The interview was over. As soon as it hit the airwaves, protesters swarmed back into the streets in larger, louder, angrier masses.

March 20: The vernal equinox began one year to the day of the sky animals' dissension. As Earth rotated on its axis and spring's first day began anew, each successive longitudinal segment was illuminated and for once, worldwide, dawn displayed perfect glorious weather of sunshine, turquoise skies and titanium-white clouds. The day started where it always started in Greenwich, England, at prime meridian, zero degrees longitude. There, scientists marked the planet's beginning of each new day at midnight, and that was when and where more very strange things began to happen.

Old Bill Davenport, a stout-bodied security guard at The Royal Observatory in Greenwich, was first. He started feeling peculiar as he plodded along the usual path of his midnight patrol around the Observatory's park-like environs. Perhaps it was a touch of indigestion from the three-day-old bangers and mash his partner had packed up for his dinner that was making him feel light headed. He stepped over the prime meridian line at Latitude 51° 28' 38' and Longitude 0° 00' 00' which was precisely marked out with a long metal railing inset into the ground so tourists could take selfies next to or straddling it, the very place the whole world's day began and ended.

One foot on one side of the rail, the other on the opposing, old Bill gasped and said, 'My word!' and very slowly, gently began floating upward as sky animals the world over said, 'So long. Nice knowing you!'

Old Bill grabbed his cell phone from its holster looped to his belt and punched in the numbers for the Greenwich West Metropolitan Police Service. Panicked, it wasn't until the third attempt he finally got the number right, but the police were of no use for he could see them away below, floating up behind him. Bumfuzzled, he dropped his phone and it tumbled downward hitting Chief Constable Birdwhistle on his noggin eliciting a distant 'Blimey!'

So, it went all around the world as longitude by longitude, one by hundreds by thousands by millions, humanity began sailing skyward. Entire planes halted in mid-flight to float up to…where? Where were they going? 'Where are we going?' People spoke to each other as higher they went. 'What is happening?' 'Are you getting cold?' 'I have vertigo!' 'Mommy, I wasn't done going potty!' Those trapped indoors found themselves scudding across ceilings of their homes and offices and domed sports stadiums, but all eventually made it outside to drift like children's balloons slowly upward into the firmament, for what was the point of remaining stuck indoors on a ceiling? Vehicles, trains, subways slowed to a dead stop with the same ultimate result for the people inside.

No one was left to wonder where they'd all gone so it did not matter. Then came March 21, and Earth was quieter than it had been in a very long time. With all humans gone, Earth did what it had always done, animals and insects what they had always done. Centuries passed, human things broke down, rusted, eroded, corroded, and what had once been dust became dust again leaving nary a human trace.

SKY DOGS EVENTUALLY interbred with Earth dogs, sky cats with Earth cats, with evolution greatly improving the intelligence of both canine and feline populations. Dogs were very pleased with the way things turned out, cats not so much because the canines, superior in brute strength, came to rule the world. Cats, aloof as they'd always seemed to be, pretended they couldn't be bothered with governmental inanities though they quietly harbored a deep resentment against the dogs who had proven to be oppressive rulers in extreme. Example: all catnip factories were shuttered by order of the Great Spoolie.

A millennium passed. In the thousand and first year, day one of spring arrived and slowly, delicately, humans began descending from wherever they'd been up in the skies. They'd lost their superior intelligence as well as their ability to speak sensically. Uppity dogs adopted some of the better looking humans as pets after doing the responsible thing, having them spade and neutered because the humans bred like, well, humans. As things progressed, dogs held human shows in which the more athletic and better looking people were trotted around a ring by trainers, showing off their physiques and walking abilities. Less-attractive humans were sent to impounds where benevolent dogs rescued them. Those humans not rescued were either entered in the World's Ugliest Human Contest or dealt with in an unkind fashion that need not be recorded here.

The only sound the sky humans could make was 'Don't even think about it!' which exasperated all dogs because they didn't know what it was they weren't supposed to think about. It took forever to break a human of that annoying habit. When the humans became extra-excited or afraid of something, they got down on their haunches and said it much louder and with great enthusiasm: 'DON'T EVEN THINK ABOUT IT! DON'T EVEN THINK ABOUT IT! DON'T EVEN THINK ABOUT IT!' pointing directly at their dog master which colossally aggravated the dogs because the humans did it every time the dogs needed to go to the bathroom. How could they know such a thing? And when a whole pack of the humans got going with the 'Don't even think about its!' in simultaneous chorus, it was beyond vexatious for the dogs, inciting them to bay at the moon or sun depending upon the time.

Some people owners paid human trainers exorbitant fees to re-program the more frequently offending 'Don't even think about it!' humans which involved shock collars. More holistic people-trainers employed collars that sprayed a certain scent humans hated called 'public bathroom' whenever a 'Don't even think about it!' was spoken. Cats ignored the silly humans just as they always had, going about their cat business in their usual detached antisocial way though they secretly enjoyed how upset the humans could make the dogs which further galled the dogs because when the cats were happy about the whole 'Don't even think about it!' thing, they began purring with a look of great satisfaction as though they'd cornered a mouse.

One day a tomcat, an indentured servant to the court appropriately named Tomcat, mewed out a 'Don't even think about it' directly to King Spoolie XX. The shocking insult proved a bad move. The King had had it with the cats and declared all-out war on the feline population. An ugly, decades-long affair ensued with countless lives lost on both sides including that of the latest Spoolie. He was assassinated by Tomcat who'd snuck a chicken bone in the King's kibbles provoking death by choking. Finally, exhausted by war, both parties agreed to a ceasefire that lasted for only a day. Then, war broke out again. And again. And again. And again.

This, then, is the true and unvarnished recordation of how dogs came to rule the world. With the first spring day of a new millennium dawning tomorrow, it is a history best not forgot.

Love is Many Things, None of them Logical

Hannah Storm

1. As You Wish

It's been snowing for days. School is cancelled and I'm dying to make a snow angel. 'It'll be the death of you', my host mother Lori warns me, putting on *The Princess Bride* for the fifth time. Lori doesn't know I lost my virginity last week on Valentines. I doubt she really knows what love is, even though she's had six children. 'Life isn't fair, it's just fairer than death', I whisper. Buttercup and Westley get it.

2. Inconceivable

I'm drinking a tiny coffee in a café, watching the boats bob in the blue Adriatic, planning the next stage of my solo trip. My eyes turn to the TV above the bar and in that split second a plane flies into a tower and someone says 'holy fuck'. I book the next boat to Venice, unsure if

I'll get there for my honeymoon, and not prepared to wait.

3. This is true love. Do you think this happens every day?

The man's back is turned. Without seeing his face, I know I'm in love. His right hand is stuffed inside the carcass of a chicken or turkey. His blonde curls bob with concentration, and his left foot rises and falls, keeping rhythm with music I can't hear, but know will form the soundtrack to our future.

4. Since the invention of the kiss

Your mouth is on mine and you kiss me like you have not eaten for one hundred days. Your lips taste like liquorice and my mouth melts into yours. We devour the Ben and Jerry's, then you scrape the bottom of the tub and smear it over my flat stomach. When you lick it off, you spin circles with your tongue, look up at me, eyes sated, and say, 'If it's twins, let's call them Cookies and Cream.'

5. You fell victim to one of the classic blunders

Cochabamba is jungle hot. The sweat slips behind my thin shirt and pools in my pants. The lights of the hotel fizz and burn and my belly aches from the Bolivian street food, even though I regretted buying it from the first bite. I climb onto the hotel treadmill, turn up the speed, worry about a power cut, watch the numbers get higher and higher, listen to the beating of my feet like drums, stop counting, fall back off the machine into the cool concrete wall. In three days, I will know it wasn't the food.

6. We'll never survive. Nonsense, you're only saying that because no one ever has.

The militia march past, a ragged battalion of men in borrowed fatigues. We are squeezed beneath the table in the house, our hosts sitting closest to the blown-out window. Sarah is the only journalist with a Kevlar helmet and I'm half in and out and under the wooden table when the roof starts to shake. A trickle become a torrent, and I scream my children's names, but all that falls from my mouth is dust.

How to Hold an Umbrella

Caroline Greene

'LIKE THIS,' SAYS Raffa, tipping the opened shell, spoke-ends towards the wall. This way, he says, people can pass in the alleys, without danger to eyes, or face. She watches from the portico as two pedestrians approach each other under the rain. They tilt their umbrellas in, back-to-back inverted commas, the curves brushing each other gently in a snippet of conversation.

The autumn sweeps by in one downpour after another. She and Raffa wade through swirling streets and clomp along the boardwalks laid out against the floods. Once, hurrying to meet him, she knocks into a jellyfish, its tendrils swaying lifeless in the rising water.

She leaves umbrellas everywhere. She takes the bus out of the city during a thunderstorm but returns under a brand new sun that sparkles from every dripping branch, so she forgets the red umbrella rolled under her feet. She loses a battle in the piazza when the wind whips up under a black brolly that is already pulling her the wrong way. In a flurry, the skin is ripped back over the spokes and it flumps to the ground, where she abandons it. The tattered skeleton skims away over the square in seconds.

'Don't lose this one,' Raffa says, as he hands her a carved handle peeping out from paper wrapping. She recognises it from Stefanelli's shop window.

'It's to keep you dry in England,' he says, rattling on, looking at his feet, leaning in to her.

All this she remembers now, years later, as she studies Raffaele's postings, as she taps the photographs he is sending out from a world in protest, as she pulls them open to fill her own screen. There, tipped against the jets from water canons, are so many umbrellas – black, tartan, branded, striped – unfurled in another autumn, not against rain this time, or floods, or swirling wind.

'Hang on to them,' she wants to tell those figures almost swamped by spray and by mists of gas from the canisters. 'Hang on.' And she wonders at their tenacity, wonders why it is something she never had, hopes, once again, that they will hold fast.

Buried

Emily Harrison

SHE ASKS YOU if you want to make another baby, taking your left hand and pushing it down the front of her pyjama shorts. She curls your fingers under hers, so they're positioned to reach inside. Her breath is sour from sleep, and you tell her, whispered, *that's not how our biology works.*

Before had been medical. Appointments and donors. Fertility and insemination. Leaflets for same sex couples.

Humming, she takes the velvety flesh of your jaw between her teeth and bites. *Let's try anyway* she says with a mouthful. *Another baby.* Her hand is still covering yours, and she cants her hips to meet the tangle of fingers. *That's what I want.* She's using her slow voice to coax, dragging out each vowel, each consonant, until they slide from her tongue to stretch and snap. You want it. A baby. And her. Just not like this. Besides, it's not something you can give.

She goes to nibble the lobe of your ear, but you falter

and tilt back. In the room above, someone slams their hotel door.

***

SHE IS RETICENT in the passenger seat, cheek turned towards the red dust desert. You'd decided on the trip together – Alice Springs to Adelaide. Open road and endless space. Turns out claustrophobia reaches the widest expanses.

When you stop at Marla, fuelling up before parking at Travellers' Rest, she is stiff and restless. She browses the understocked supermarket so she can stretch her legs before taking over the driving. You sip your bitter takeout coffee and follow her path like a lamb.

***

IT WAS NOT her fault. *There was no time to swerve.* Fresh blood marks the bumper. Her hands. Face. It's on you too. The mother is nowhere in sight, but the kangaroo is clearly a baby. They don't usually leave the pouch until they're at least six months old.

Knelt in near prayer between tarmac and dirt, she cradles its carcass and refuses to let its body go. You try to pry at her forearm – *don't*. Helplessly you remain, your hand soft on her skin.

Do you want to bury it? You ask, after ten minutes has passed. She has been suspended in silence, brushing tender thumb strokes across its fur. The sun is hot, and you need to start moving. *There's a shov —*

Her she interrupts, wet eyes staring you down. *It's a her.*

Behind the boot you throw up your belly and wipe your mouth on your t-shirt. The yellowy stain of sick smudges the cotton.

With heavy arms you reach for the shovel that's wedged between your suitcases. There's an emergency foil blanket and a metal jack too. When you return the joey is laid to her side, curled up as though it could be alive and dreaming.

Down in the dirt her hands are clawing — pulling up the earth. You crumple down next to her, letting the shovel clatter to the road. Together you keep digging.

Mess of Love

Jason Jackson

WHEN SHE WAS a young woman, Rachel had a thing for strength. The boys she knew were becoming men, and at the lido she'd watch as they strutted around the water, pushing each other in. It was their bodies she was drawn to: their shoulders, their biceps, their hands. Sometimes they'd try to grab her but she always avoided their grasp, until the time a boy she didn't know caught hold of her and picked her up off the wet tiles. He tossed her through the air and she fell like a flailing bird, hitting the water hard. She was submerged in silence, as if life above the surface had ceased and it was only her that could ever change. She always felt this separation when she dived in, but there was more to it this time. She'd been *thrown*. She was underwater not through her own volition but through another's will, and there was something thrilling about the acceptance of it. She wanted to stay where she was precisely because someone else had put her there, and by staying submerged she was saying to him, *See? You did this. You're capable of changing the world. You can do whatever you want.* She held her breath, her eyes closed, and she was strong. She imagined him on the surface, watching. She knew that the longer she stayed down there, the more he'd want her.

She turned in the water and kicked towards the bottom. Long seconds passed as she thought about the feel of his hands grabbing her waist, lifting her from the tiles. Finally, beyond breathless, she pushed for the surface and came up for air.

She looked for him amongst the crowd, and there he was, the water giving a sheen to his skin, the sun-shadows playing around the curves of his arms and his neck. He still hadn't seen her through the chaos of heads and arms and bodies which was the lido that hot summer. He was scanning the water towards the deep end, so she began to wave. She didn't want to shout, and anyway, she didn't know his name. He saw her, held his hands above his head and dived in.

Later, in the cool of the early evening, he kissed her against the wire mesh fence which ran around the perimeter of the lido. It bowed backwards with their weight, and as she held onto him she could feel the solid slab of his torso.

She closed her eyes, lost.

***

IT TOOK FIVE years of marriage for him to run fat, to lose his definition and shape. In the mornings, as he lifted himself from the bed and stood gurning into the wardrobe mirror, Rachel watched the burgeoning thickness around his waist, the heavy set of his buttocks. His step on the stairs was certain, deliberate, and there was a weight to him when he lay on top of her, taking his time, pushing himself up above her, holding himself there, then moving slowly into her and out again. *Pressy-ups* he called it. 'How many d'ya think I can get to tonight?' he'd say, and she'd play along with the game.

Her mother had warned her. 'He'll break you,' she said. 'A man like that.' She was wrong, of course, but she died swearing she'd be proved right. Rachel let her believe it, because things were easier that way, but it hurt. Her own mother. No faith. People didn't understand: for something to break there had to be resistance.

He would never lift a hand to harm anyone, that's what he always said. And it was true. Those times when she was late with the dinner, coming out of a steam-filled kitchen to his sighs and his hard, heavy look, she'd see his fists clenched around his knife and fork. She'd see the whitened knuckles, the callouses at the joints of each thumb. The force of just one blow could kill someone. She'd heard stories of women punched so hard they hit their heads on cooker-corners, door-handles, concrete floors. There was a woman called Mary at work, with her blackened eyes and excuses. Everyone knew. Rachel had met Mary's husband at a party once, been introduced to him. She watched as he lifted his hand time and again to move Mary's hair from her shoulders or to place a palm in the small of her back. She saw his dirtied, bitten-down fingernails as he squeezed Mary's hand.

There were times when Nick's grip could be too tight, when he held onto her longer than necessary. One night on their honeymoon they were sitting across from each other at a table in a restaurant, and as she stood up to go to the ladies he kept hold of her hand. She laughed, trying to pull away from his grip, but he only tightened it. To keep pulling was useless; he wouldn't let her go, whatever she did. There was a strange kind of victory about the act of giving in, of allowing herself to become loose. It was defiance as well as submission. She let her arm slacken, her body slump back into the chair, and her eyes never left his as she opened herself inside, waited, and finally felt the warmth and the wetness, heard the drip of it as it seeped through her dress, onto the chair and the tiled floor of the restaurant.

He realised what she was doing, and shaking his head he stood up, lifted her from the chair, cradled her in his arms and carried her from the bar, both of them laughing hysterically.

Back at the hotel, they showered together. When he nuzzled at her like a calf with its mother, she stroked his head, saying, 'I'll never leave you, baby. I'll never, ever leave you.'

***

IN THOSE FIRST years of marriage, she offered her acquiescence as a gift, and he accept it without a thought. They often went grocery shopping together, and he made the choices, silently nodding or frowning as she picked things from the shelves. Sometimes she anticipated his preferences based on weeks and months of experience, but for no reason his expected nod would be a frown, so she'd put back the usual tin of beans, the usual toilet roll, the usual cereal, and select others at random until he closed his eyes, inclined his head, smiled that full-lipped smile.

Driving was necessarily her responsibility, as he'd never learned, never even taken lessons. On longer journeys—when they drove out to the coast early on summer weekend mornings, or when they went north to see his sick mother—he'd sit passively in the passenger seat, seemingly asleep, his hand resting on her thigh. Sometimes she'd take a corner too quickly, and his grip would tighten, those thick fingers pushing directly against nerve endings, seeking out the sinews and the inevitable resistances of bone. Nothing would be said. There would be sharp breaths. There would be sighs, and she would feel his fear at his lack of control. His hand would grip, his fingers tighten, until he deemed things to be more acceptable, and then he would relax, his hand resting lightly on her thigh once again.

On occasion, this would leave bruises. She remembered once huddling with him under the duvet in the pushed-together single beds of his mother's spare room. He pulled up her thin night-dress, bending his head to lap at her skin where the darkened marks were already forming. She stroked his head, her hands in his hair, pulling at it, and he made sounds which could only be understood as despair. He pushed inside her, and as she held onto the thickness of his arms she thought of his mother lying awake, listening to the news on the radio in the room next door. When she bit into his shoulder, he shook her off with a grunt and she whispered in his ear, 'You can do anything to me, baby. Anything at all.' He quickened, finished, then turned over to sleep while she watched the grey of the room, the shadows, the subtle light which seemed to seep in from nowhere.

***

IT WAS LESS than a year later—a bright summer morning in a private ward—that Rachel listened as Nick's mother outlined how things would be now the initial exhilaration of their marriage was gone, how there would be nothing to replace it other than a series of mundane, undeniable disappointments.

'There might not be a big thing,' she said, her bird-hands resting on the stiff hospital bedsheets. 'There doesn't always have to be an affair. But you know him. He'll never be satisfied.' She turned towards the light coming through the blinds. 'He doesn't want children, does he?'

Rachel sighed, looking at the door and willing Nick to return with her coffee. 'There's time.'

His mother made a noise which could once have been laughter. 'A man like that? Don't you see? *He's* your child, dear. He's not the kind to be second-best.'

She was dead within six months—painfully, fighting every inch of the way—and on the night after the funeral, Rachel held Nick as he slept. Lying there in the house where her husband had spent his childhood, she thought of her own family, her mother, the quiet voice and the heavy-lidded eyes. There had been small attentions and brief moments of love between them but nothing Rachel could hold onto in the dark. Her mother had been distant, her father too. She'd never seen her parents touch each other, had never heard them argue. There'd been a stillness to their lives together which Rachel was only able to define as coldness once her mother's cancer killed her, three short months after an initially hopeful diagnosis.

She tried to imagine Nick becoming so ill he could die. She looked at him—his arm flung clumsily across her where it pressed down on her breast—and she tried to imagine him holding a child, how he would be full of the undeniable confusions and messes of love. Eventually, she turned over, moving Nick's arm gently from her as she shifted across in the bed and closed her eyes.

***

BEYOND WHAT NICK'S mother had called the initial exhilaration, the marriage continued, and Rachel often imagined they were borne aloft on Nick's physical strength alone, as if he were carrying them through the world. She felt herself physically subsumed by him, the way he hovered over her, the way he wrapped her close when they were outside in the wind or the rain. Sometimes, she'd grip the flesh of him, its hardness, and she'd have to close her eyes and take a breath. She listened to him less and less, and he said little anyway, their conversations consisting of his short pronouncements to which she would agree with a smile or a nod or, sometimes, a small kiss on his cheek. In this way she felt somehow like a mother and a daughter at the same time—much more these two than a wife, anyway—and with this came the understanding that there were small things about Nick which disappointed her as a daughter could be disappointed in a father, or a mother a son.

One morning, she watched him lifting sacks of bedding-soil to use on their garden. There were twenty sacks on the truck parked outside, and Nick and the delivery man were working in a metronomic rhythm to unload everything quickly in torrential rain. Rachel watched from the front room, and Nick's easy grip, his nonchalant strength, disgusted her. How simple it seemed, this to-and-fro, how ridiculous. Was this all Nick could do? Suddenly, one of the sacks which the delivery man had thrown from the back of the truck burst apart as Nick caught it, and the soil spilt everywhere. He laughed, and as he turned around to face her she saw the streaks of brown soil turning to mud down the front of his sodden white T-shirt. He was grinning, and she had to turn away from this childlike thing, this mud-monster, as she felt the vomit rise in her throat.

It was the first sign of the pregnancy. She found herself unable to tell Nick, and this led her to realise that he was not strong. He was physical. He was hard and tough and solid. But he was a child: simple and coarse. Or he was like her father: uninterested in anything other than self-affirmation. He was her husband, and she knew he loved her. But his love was unthinking. If it were to be faced with anything other than simple acquiescence, with straightforward reciprocation, she knew it would quickly become something else.

Other moments in the following month brought her quietly to tears: the Saturday when he took her to the circus and couldn't stop laughing at the clowns when all she could do was stare at the dishevelled, slowly swaying elephant; the evening when, walking home drunk from a restaurant, he suddenly lifted her up, ran across the road with her and put her, feet-first, into a waste-bin, laughing all the while; the slow weekday nights when he fell asleep on the couch, sitting upright, jaw hanging loose, t-shirt pulled askew and a noise coming from him, low, rasping and inhuman.

There were days when she could convince herself that the breadth of his shoulders as he undressed, the slabs of his biceps as he held himself above her and the thick cords of sinew in his neck as he turned away were enough. His strength was real and deep. Six weeks, eight weeks, ten, all passed. In the midst of a growing feeling of giddiness, expectation and a notion that all the years leading up to this had been nothing more than prologue, she told him.

She made a dish he loved: grilled chicken, charred green peppers, cumin. As she put out the steaming plates she said, quietly, that she was pregnant.

'How long are you gone?' he said.

'Almost eleven weeks, now.'

He lifted a forkful to his mouth and blew gently. 'And there's nothing we can do?'

'Nick, I want this baby.'

'You never said you wanted one before.'

It was true. She'd always taken her pill. The only time they'd talked of children was before they were married, and that had been to laugh off the idea as something too adult, too far beyond them. It was only now she found this absurd. How could they not have talked about this? How could she not have demanded it?

'Can you be glad for us?' she said.

'Let's see,' was all he said to that.

Later, she was upstairs taking a bath and he came into the room. This bathing had become a nightly routine, and she kept the water tepid and deep so that she was almost entirely submerged, her knees sticking up like two small islands amongst the bubbles. It wasn't unusual for Nick to come into the bathroom at these times, and sometimes he joined her in the bath, sitting behind her so that she was cradled in his thighs with the water almost spilling over the sides. But this time he hovered in the doorway.

'I love how you never knock,' she said. It was meant playfully, an attempt to move beyond the sourness of their mealtime, and as she looked at the shape of him, his arms held at his sides, she was aware of his bulk, a weight with potential.

He said nothing. There was a sadness to the set of his mouth as he walked slowly to her, knelt at the side of the bath and placed his hand lightly on her forehead. It was a move she was used to, an affectation. He'd always found it difficult to touch her tenderly, and this gesture— something a child might do when playing doctors and nurses, a parody of temperature-taking—had become his only way of reaching out to her with anything other than sexual want.

She held his gaze, took hold of his wrist, and he smiled as she slowly sank beneath the surface.

Under the water was another world. There was the distant presence of him, and her acceptance that while she stayed submerged, nothing would change. It was like a rock in her hand, this knowledge; she knew how to use it, how to hurt him with it. How to love him too.

She thought about the day they met, the day he threw her into the pool. She remembered the echoed distance of the sounds, her own almost-weightlessness, the desperation to rise, the pull to stay. Now, underwater again, she listened for a heartbeat other than her own—the quicker, softer, weaker one hidden somewhere deep inside of her—and as she held onto Nick's wrist she waited a moment before rising up into their changed, unfathomable world.

Strawberries

Clare Zinkin

A PERSON CANNOT read a book whilst hulling strawberries. A maxim my mother discovered to her chagrin when she sliced off her thumb one summer's morning. The knife was so sharp, the slice so complete, that she didn't notice her thumb had detached until out of the corner of her eye she spied blood staining the berries an even brighter red. The book in question was *Anna Karenina* and my mother always said that it was the 'really good bit', although I didn't believe her because her nose was always in a book, bad bits and all.

She read while waiting in hospital triage too, her thumb packed in ancient ice cubes in a sandwich Tupperware on my lap, her left hand bandaged with thick wads of kitchen towel, her right hand holding *Anna*. I squirmed next to her, the plastic chair sticking with petulant wilfulness so that when her name was finally called, I had to peel my thigh carefully from the seat lest the skin remain melded to the plastic.

Her thumb never looked the same afterwards; it had a jagged scar across the join and sat slightly skewwhiff as if she was always hitchhiking. It was the reason my father left her too, my grandmother said. Not the skewwhiff thumb, but the reading. Apparently, it was unreasonable behaviour to always have one's head in a book.

I didn't mind the books. When my mother read, I read too. She read propped against the Formica-coated counter waiting for the toast to pop, and I read at the kitchen table, eating raspberry yogurt. She read out loud to me when I was in the shower, shouting her words over the cascade of water. I knew she had her nose in a book whilst walking to school pick up because on the way home she stuck her good thumb in the pages to mark her place. We talked about what I was reading at school, but if I was uncommunicative, she'd regurgitate the story she'd been reading instead. It was surprising how often I had little to say about my day, especially when she was reading about the French woman who cheated on her husband and then poisoned herself. Or the woman who went mad staring at yellow wallpaper. And the adventures of Scarlett O'Hara were ingrained in my soul. My mother retold every story to me; she didn't believe that books should be categorised by age. All books were for all humans, she said. And your father was never one of those.

Her books were borrowed from the library, and they had dirty plastic covers, ripped at the spine and top so that they were serrated and dangerous and you could cut your thumb on them. The contents were dangerous too, women kept in attics and revengeful girls with telekinetic powers. They emitted a smell when you opened them, a smell I liked as much as the contents, a sort of musty usedness that made me think of old grandmas with grey buns and knitting needles, of kindly old men who sat and read newspapers in the middle of the day. My mother turned down the pages where she had paused reading, and commented on where others had done the same. A sort of historical reading footprint, giving each book its own unique identity. The librarian didn't approve, she used to examine the books we returned for folded corners – she's got my number, my mother said. After that, we put the books in the outside returns box.

I think I was in Year 4 when they closed down the library, selling off the stock, and turning the building into luxury flats. We rehoused a good deal of the books, supplementing the library's 20p finds with £1 books from the charity shop. My mother said the difference in price represented the attitude they held towards their clientele. The library was for the dispossessed and positively desperate. The charity shops were for opportunists, she said, the word dripping from her mouth like a slug's trail of slime.

She took to taking books to the till with the clothes she wanted, their threads shimmering ruby-red and cerise, my mother haggling with the volunteer to throw in a book with the scarlet textiles. As we left, making our way past the discarded plastic toys, the china that had served too many dinners, I asked her if she thought that requesting a free book with a clothes purchase as if it was a BOGOF in a supermarket, was opportunism. She said it was savviness. Thinking back, I'm not sure any of the charity shop customers were opportunists. The shop had the same musty smell as the library, but whereas the library was comforting and woolly, like a dog come in from the rain, the shop's mustiness held a rejected air, a sadness. Death was in reach.

Eventually we had so many dispossessed paperbacks that my mother suggested we build a den with them in the middle of the living room. It took us a whole day, while the rain slashed diagonally against the kitchen window, and plopped impolitely from the leaking roof onto the floor next to the toilet as if it were a small boy urinating with distinctly bad aim. Or a big boy, my mother said, shaking her head. It's not as if your father ever hit the target.

We laid a first tier on the floor, blueprinting the den. It was filled with Barbara Taylor Bradford books, with bare-chested men facing up. My mother shook her head, they should be the top layer, she said, stroking one worn cover with her gnarly thumb. We placed another layer over the top, on and on, overlapping for strength, and after we had amassed walls 20 books high, we agreed they should be double layered for extra resilience, and we went around the outside stacking more. Luckily my father had taken the sofa with him, so it was only a case of shifting the bean bag into our bedroom and moving stray mugs from the floor. By teatime there was a den large and tall enough for me to crawl into and sit cross-legged with a book of my own, a torch, and a bowl of strawberries. We hadn't made the entrance big enough, my mother's hips made the sides wobble when she tried to shimmy inside, and although she was thinner by this point – strawberries don't hold as many calories as a plate of digestive biscuits – she was still too big a person to fit. The next day the book she wanted to read was halfway up the front wall, and when she took it down, the whole thing caved in upon itself like a marriage disintegrating. After that we got used to living amongst the rubble of our earthquake-stricken den – books carpeted the floor, there was danger in sliding on their peeling covers.

By summertime, my mother had read all of what had been the front wall of books. She started on the side wall in the evenings, sat on the balcony of our flat. It was a tiny space – a lick of tarmac with iron railings and nailed-in clear plastic at the top to stop toddlers sticking their heads through or diving over. The sun hit the tarmac in the afternoons, two hours of glaring sunshine before it moved on, and we sat with our backs against the scorching bricks, the tarmac hot against our bare legs, picking cherries from a paper bag, popping the fruits off their stems with our teeth, then chewing hard and sucking the stone until every facet of fruit was removed, and the stone was smooth and unblemished. Some things were worth spending money on, she said. I liked the sweetness, the juiciness popping in my mouth, but I liked best when we spat out the stones afterwards, watching them career through the gaps at the bottom of the railings, like pinballs in slots, then plummeting thirty-two floors to sudden death. My mother and I high-fived every time the cherry stone bounced straight through.

Having cherries mid-afternoon meant no tea – there was only so much money for food and cherries were expensive, even the bruised ones from the Bengalese man at the minimart two doors down from Tesco metro. He had started selling vegetables and fruit on the pavement, but moved into the rental space when the butchers closed down. If you sniffed really hard you could still smell the ferrous scent when picking the least bruised apples from the pile. Just the Red Delicious or Pink Lady for us. My mother picked red chillies, red peppers, red onions. She scooped the red lentils from the bucket with an oversize ladle and they dropped into her paper bag like the cherry stones raining on concrete. Hot chilli lentil stew made for a fiery tea.

One time she brought home a watermelon, vivid

green on the outside, but such a surprise when she thwacked it hard with the meat cleaver, sending black pips ricocheting off the kitchen walls and a light red residue splattering our hair and clothes and the already stained walls.

We ate tinned tomatoes, raw salted radishes, beetroots roasted until their juices bled, overly sweet processed strawberry jam that was more like runny syrup. I looked longingly at the brand with the French style cap, made to look as if it were homemade – with real strawberries suspended in the gelatinous spread. My mother put crisps in the shopping basket too – Walkers ready salted in their red crinkly packets. Strawberry ice cream, cranberry juice, useful in so many ways, my mother said.

Sometime after the strawberry hulling incident, I saw a poster on the bus for audio books, and implored my mother to invest in some kind of electronic contraption, listening as a safer option. She wouldn't hear of it though, dismissing the concept as not really reading, and anyway, she laughed, that isn't the kind of thing the charity shops sell.

By then she was reading *The Awakening* by Kate Chopin, and her mood was brightening. She took to smearing red lipstick across her dry lips in case of visitors. But there were none. My father had long since stopped popping round to see me, and I never invited anyone from school, in case they wondered why we had books instead of furniture, and only tinned tomatoes in the cupboard.

If it hadn't been for school dinners, I might have turned a little red myself. To compensate for the diet at home, I eschewed ketchup at school, opting instead for mayonnaise with my chips, cheese or tuna with my jacket potato instead of baked beans.

Red dominated our days, from cherries and gloopy tomato-drenched spaghetti hoops, to the redness in my face when my mother picked me up at the school gates instead of letting me walk home by myself. We rode the red bus to the end of town and back for something to do. The local football team donned a red kit, and my mother took pleasure being out and about on match days, walking the streets and milling with the red scarf-wearing crowds, their banners draping the town crimson.

We watched sunsets from the balcony. I was so high I imagined I could lean over the plastic and touch the red ball. My mother's face reflected its pink glow, like the Pink Lady apples we bought from the Bengalese man. Red sky at night meant shepherd's delight, and the sun would shine on us the following day.

But red sky in the morning was a warning.

Was it portent, the day the sun bled red between clammy clouds as I walked to school, the air so heavy it felt as if I were walking into a solid wall with each step? The sun carried on bleeding a deep rouge between layers of low purple cloud the whole way through assembly, until grey clouds flooded in mid-morning, obliterating the rosy sky just as my father had greyed my mother's days.

It wasn't the red car, although that should have taken her. My mother was reading *The Bell Jar*, and when a fellow pedestrian picked it up from where it lay splayed on the road, unseemly against the black tarmac, it was open to page 134. My mother had been knocked, clipped by the car at the crossing, when she failed to observe its approach. A red gash above her eye from her collision with the road, a warning that walking with one's nose in a book wasn't acceptable behaviour, even at a pelican crossing.

We had beans on toast for supper, reading side by side, the ketchup adding even darker splodges of red to the plate. Mine matched my red school jumper, my mother's plate matched her injury – the burnt toast crumbs like flecks of tarmac in a bleeding wound of beans. Then bed as usual, side by side, reading before lights out.

Orangey red colours look darker against a night sky. The flames took more quickly to our flat than the others, devouring the discarded books from our dilapidated den as if they were coals in a stately home's fireplace. Curling flames lit scarlet, saffron and amber, powering up the walls. Whoosh, the red light growing and growing, mirrored in the red flashing lights from the red fire engine outside. She didn't hear my coughing, my screaming – the red pills had made sure of that. I tried to pull her heavy body from her bed, but it was like the watermelon – too heavy to shift, and I had to roll her dead weight onto the floor. The heat prickled my skin; it was different to sunshine on tarmac – this heat was redder, rawer, drier. It parched my throat, scratching at my hands.

The top floor was good for chucking cherry stones, less equipped for escape. I heard crashing as the flames toppled belongings, the shrieks of my neighbours, the whining of sirens. I rolled my mother over and over, but the bedroom doorway was as impenetrable as the doorway had been to our book den. She just wouldn't roll through.

In the end, I left her, in her Santa-red pyjamas studded with green fir trees and brown reindeer, and I ran out and up to the roof hatch, past the glass-fronted red fire alarm that someone had smashed, the glass puncturing my bare feet with tiny scars. I winced and hopped all the way up the grey stone steps to the roof, where the city lay stretched out in a spectrum of vermillion from the taillights of cars to the traffic lights along the roads; and a red helicopter whup-whupped above, its dangling ladder like a cat's tail.

I don't eat strawberries anymore. Cherries make me sick, and my toast is covered with a thin layer of honey – no jam. I keep reading though; sometimes while I'm in the bath, and sometimes even when I'm walking down the road to pick up my daughter from school. The ear buds are almost invisible nowadays, technology makes everything so small. And the voices – sometimes I pick a book simply because of the actor narrating it. Although no one has yet come close to the expression and emotion my mother put into her stories, as if she were inflecting each word with a different colour.

Load More Comments...

Jan Barker

December

A PULITZER JOURNALIST wouldn't lose sleep over it. I had turned in the critical word-count but my article in The Echo carried no trace of the sweat lost in crafting an appropriately uncaring tone. I eased off one heel to irritate a blister while I raked through the detail, caressing a large glass of Shiraz and the high view over Lincoln's winter lights from the bar of the Bishop's Palace.

'A man died yesterday after being hit by a train travelling between Nottingham and Lincoln. The incident happened at 12.32pm by the Bleasby foot crossing. A British Transport Police spokesperson said the victim, pronounced dead at the scene, was identified as Freddy Bryce, 39, who lived alone in nearby Fiskerton. The Coroner's Office has been informed.'

***

January

Freddy Bryce: *Thanks for your messages. I'm doing all right. How is everyone? Up to no good?*

Comments:

➢ *Bryce, mate, such a relief to hear you. We used to knock around the estate when we were kids, remember? Sorry to hear your news, glad you're still on Facebook. RIP mate.*

➢ *Lovey, we missed you at Christmas. We gave the boys a tow-truck from Uncle Freddy, you'd have loved it.*

➢ *WTF? A grown man and you don't know how to cross a railway line in one piece?*

Replies:

➢ *How can you be so insensitive? Who are you to judge!*

➢ *Get off this page if you can't say anything nice.*

➢ *Moron!*

[Load More Comments …]

***

February

Notes of Coroner's Hearing 11th February.

Freddy Bryce. Flat 14 Delphi Tower, Fiskerton. 39. Single.

G.P: Mr Bryce had 'intermittent mental health issues.' Irregular use of medication. Largely self-managed.
(But not 'self-managed' terribly well, eh?)

Boss: Manicured ginger beard. Freddy learned to cook in the Navy. Part-time sous-chef, Pirlo's, Lincoln. Always spilling things. Took time off sick in December, busiest time. Commuted by train *(of course).*

Police: Incident treated as 'non-suspicious'. A note on brown paper found in remains of a trouser pocket. Three words scratched and bloodstained. *Peace at last.*
(Corny, Freddy, a disappointing cliché. Could have done better than that.)

Train driver: Stumbles through recall. Applied emergency brakes, alerted signaller. No time to sound the horn. Procedure followed exactly. Then unable to move until the guard led him away from the cab.

'You don't expect to go to work and help end someone's life... you can't swerve, you watch it happen... if you see a cow ahead on the line – you've time to stop then, it takes time...

But this bloke, he came out from the crossing like a spring. Then he's just parts on the track... I wake up feeling the impact, hearing the noise, you know, the crunch.'

(Poor bugger, looks like hell. Selfish of you, Freddy, selfish.)

Overweight neighbour: Fixing a radiator leak, saw Freddy day before he died. 'He said hello, seemed fine.' *(Where do they get these people? Obviously not 'fine'!)*

Rail Accident Investigator: earnest woman, grey suit, red shoes. One hundred and fifteen train suicides last year. High proportion in Lincolnshire. 'It's so flat, you see.' *(No, I don't see, but Coroner nods anyway.)*

Clinical Psychologist: keeps picking the same piece of nothing off his lapel. 'I would posit that Mr Bryce was not consciously trying to die.' Ripple of morbid laughter. 'After consultation with his doctors, I believe Mr Bryce...' *(Freddy. His name was Freddy.)* '...suffered an undiagnosed condition known as Akathisia. Difficult to medicate. He'd be driven by inner agitation to such an unbearable extreme that he felt compelled to jump out of his own body to end the torture. It's not uncommon in train suicides and people who jump from heights.'

A sort-of cousin (Jean?): Freddy's elderly parents lived in Kent. Too far to travel. Shipped Freddy home for a more convenient funeral. 'I'd have liked to attend but it's a long way. Busy lives.' *('Busy'... right. Cramp in my calf. How much longer?)*

***

THE CORONER RETURNED a verdict of suicide. No surprise there. Most train-jumpers barely get a mention but Freddy deserved more. Even so, I reduced his lifetime to the required single paragraph for an inquest. Only the couples warrant more attention. Especially the elderly ones. As if it's romantic to hold hands, for better or worse, facing down a frantic train driver until parted by several tons of speeding metal.

***

March

Freddy Bryce: *Well it's been an interesting few weeks settling in and all that. How's tricks with you lot?*

Comments:

➤ *Hey Freddy! Some local journalist is after your story. Should we talk to her? You'll be famous for 15 minutes!*

Replies:

➤ *Well he's not obviously going to reply to you, is he!*

➤ *Why not, it's his story. It's up to him.*

➤ *Why do you think? He's dead, you plank.*

➤ *Look at his posts!*

> ➤ *It's just that beyond the grave thing!*

> ➤ *None of your bloody business anyway, mate.*

> ➤ *None of you should be on here. It's moronic.*

> ➤ *Yeah well, you'd know about that.*

[*Load More Comments ...*]

***

I MET THE friends in the Royal Stars, a downtrodden pub on The Cannibal – proper name The Hannibal Estate. *(Council planners, two out of ten for foresight.)*

Freddy's sort-of cousin Jean looked as though life had given up trying to get through to her. She stayed thirty-five minutes, drank Bacardi and coke like it was still the eighties.

'I thought he liked the new job. It was a decent place, better money.'

How often did you see him?

'Oh, you know, not often. Busy...you know how it is.'

A friend called Vincent fell over his words as the pub door closed behind Jean.

'She hardly knew Freddy. Only invited him Christmas so he'd buy presents for her boys. She couldn't wait to claim him on Facebook, same day he went und...well, y'know... Just grabbing attention, I reckon; bit of excitement in her sad little life. I mean, me and Kev were at school with him, weren't we, Kev? Can I get another pint? On your expenses, yeah?'

The friend called Kevin said, 'We were the only ones saw him regular. He had a decent streak, though. He gave me some plants for my bit of garden.'

'He dug those up off the roundabout, Kev,' Vincent clarified from the bar.

'Did he? Still, it's the thought. He was awkward with people he didn't know. Sort of panicked if he had to talk to anyone.'

'Restless sod, he was.' Vincent returned with a single pint.

'Yeah, he was always fidgeting, sort of nervous. You didn't bring me a pint then, Vin?'

'So,' I persevered. 'He'd signed up for Dead Social?'

'One of those,' said Kevin, 'They all do it now, social media. Posting like when he was alive.'

'Obviously like 'alive', you plank.'

Kevin and Vincent, the double act, spattered beer on the table.

'And people still talk to Freddy, months later? Think he's posting from beyond the grave?'

'It don't do no harm.'

'But when you reply, do you think Freddy's really there?'

'No, course not. We just want him to be.'

(Another soft lad, scared of being lonely when he's dead)

***

April

Freddy Bryce: *It's been wild here. I need a rest. Tell me all what you've been up to.*

Comments:

➢ *How's it going, Freddy. Miss our Navy days, don't you?*

➢ *We miss you in the Royal Stars. Keeping the old Bryce seat warm for you.*

➢ *Fair winds, mate.*

[Load more Comments...]

***

MY EDITOR LIKED the new article. 'Dead Social: Why We Leave Messages to the Dear Departed.' *'When Your Heart Stops Beating, You'll Keep Tweeting.'* (Christ in a bucket, whatever next?) I wrote about lining the pockets of "digital executors"; about cashing in on formless fears of death; about trying to stave off guilt for doing fuck all while the person was alive. But I worded it better than that. I ordered three glasses of Shiraz while I wrote it. That's how good it was.

***

Last December

THE DAY BEFORE I reported Freddy's death, I missed my connection from Nottingham to Lincoln. With a brief run, a twisted ankle in new heels, I slipped sideways through the closing doors of the 12.10pm. Solitary passenger in the front carriage slugging across frosty pancaked fenlands under silver-slate skies. Near Bleasby, I glanced ahead on the rare curve. The man wore no coat, jiggered from side to side at the foot crossing. His eyes shifted, maybe saw me in that half-second when he raised his arms as if in embrace and lunged downwards. An evaporating shadow. A single muffled thud. Freddy and I met as the wheels jolted heavily into his body beneath me. The breath shook out of his lungs and mine in much the same moment. But I breathed in again, three fingers pressed against my lips.

The two carriages convulsed to an emergency halt. Most of Freddy rested somewhere behind me, entwined with the carriage. Further beyond, a bloodied mound, shredded brown corduroy trousers, the bone that was once shin. I stared at my knees and breathed until the nausea ebbed. Didn't look again.

The guard moved swiftly to lead the pale, rigid driver away from the cab.

'I'm afraid we have struck a person.'

('Struck a person'?)

171

'This usually delays us around ninety minutes. The emergency services will be working just behind you. Best not to look.'

(You think?)

***

THE HOST OF the Regional Press Awards described my 'Dead Social' piece as original, clever, insightful. I toasted my cleverness with three glasses of Shiraz before I weaved on stage to accept my award. Now I write the feature articles and some other poor sod sits through the inquests. Freddy still keeps in touch.

Author Biographies

Jan Barker – Jan lives in Birmingham and achieved a M.A. in Creative Writing (Distinction) from Birmingham City University in 2017, following early retirement from a career in local government and the NHS. Jan's writing first loves are short fiction and theatre writing and she belongs to a local writers' group. She has previously been published by Bare Fiction magazine and hopes one day to see her stage play brought to life.

Timothy Boudreau – Timothy Boudreau lives in northern New Hampshire with his wife, Judy. His recent work appears at Storgy, Spelk, Milk Candy Review, X-R-A-Y Literary Magazine, Bending Genres and Third Point Press, and has been nominated for Best Microfiction 2020. His collection *Saturday Night and other Short Stories* is available through Hobblebush Books. Find him on Twitter at @tcboudreau or at timothyboudreau.com.

Helen Eccles – Helen Eccles writes commercial fiction. Her first novel is a domestic thriller, now set aside to 'brew' and revisit in the new year. In the meantime, she is working on ideas for novel 2 and more short stories. Helen lives near Hebden Bridge in West Yorkshire with her husband and other animals.

Louise Farr – Louise Farr is a teacher and writer from Northern Ireland.

In 2018, she was the winner of the Benedict Kiely Short Story Competition and The Trisha Ashley Award. In 2019, she won The Ink Tears Short Story Competition and The Dalkey Writing Festival Short Story Competition. She was a finalist in the 2018 and 2019 Doolin Writers' Weekend Short Story Competition and won third prize in the 2019 TSS Flash 400. She was longlisted for the 2019 Bristol Short Story Prize and shortlisted for The Bridport 2019 Short Story Prize. One of her short stories appears in *Still Worlds Turning*, an anthology of short stories published by No Alibis Press.

Geoffrey Graves – Geoffrey Kent Graves' work has appeared in Calliope Literary Journal, Ageless Authors Anthology (First Place), Short Story Project, and others. Finalist: Cutthroat's Barry Lopez Nonfiction Award, Notable Story Gemini Magazine, Honorable Mention New Millennium Writing Awards, Pinch Literary Award finalist, two Honorable Mentions Short Story American Prize, Short-listed Ireland's 2019 International Fish Memoir Prize. His film script, "Baker's Dozen," was optioned by Columbia Pictures. He worked in the script department of CBS, Television City, Hollywood.

Caroline Greene – Caroline Greene @cgreene100 is an English Language teacher who's also worked as an editor and features writer, and as a fund-raiser in the theatre. Her work has appeared in the Fish Anthology 2011, Flash Magazine, Bath Flash Fiction Vol. 3, the National Flash Fiction Day Anthology 2019, Flash Fiction Festival Anthology 3, Splonk and @FlashBack Fiction.

Emily Harrison – Emily uses writing as an escape from reality and doesn't drink enough water. She has had work published with X-R-A-Y Literary Magazine, Ellipsis Zine, Barren Magazine, STORGY Magazine, The Molotov Cocktail, Coffin Bell, Retreat West, Nymphs, Tiny Molecules and Gone Lawn to name a few. She reviews books for STORGY Magazine when she has a moment, has been shortlisted a couple of times and can be found on Twitter at @emily__harrison tweeting/retweeting nonsense. Her website is: emilyharrisonwrites.com.

Emma Hutton – Emma Hutton is an Irish writer based in London. Her stories have appeared in The Mechanics' Institute Review, Southword, Litro and Best Microfiction 2020. She won the Mairtín Crawford Short Story Award 2019 and the TSS Flash Fiction Competition 2019. Website: www.iamhutton.com/stories

Jason Jackson – Jason Jackson's prize-winning fiction has been published widely online and in print. In 2019 his work has placed in competitions including the Cranked Anvil prize, as well as featuring at The Nottingham Review and New Flash Fiction Review. At the beginning of the year, Jason's hybrid prose/photography work *The Unit* was published by A3 Press.

Niamh MacCabe – Niamh is an award-winning writer and artist published in over thirty journals and anthologies in Ireland, the U.K., and the U.S. including *The Stinging Fly, Mslexia, Wasafiri, No Alibis Press, Aesthetica, The Writer Magazine, Structo, The Bristol Prize Anthology, Skylight 47, Tears In The Fence, The Honest Ulsterman, Bare Fiction, The Lonely Crowd, The Lighthouse, Bath Flash Fiction Anthology, The Cormorant,* and *The Ogham Stone*. She lives with her sons in rural North Leitrim, Ireland. Website: niamhmaccabe.com

Bruce Meyer – Bruce Meyer is author or editor of 64 books of poetry, short fiction, flash fiction, non-fiction, and literary journalism. He was winner of the 2019 Anton Chekhov Prize for Fiction, and a finalist for the Bath Short Story Prize, the Tom Gallon Trust Fiction Prize, and winner of the Freefall Prize for Poetry. He lives in Barrie, Ontario

Sherry Morris – Originally from America's heartland, Sherry Morris writes prize-winning flash fiction and short stories from a farm in the Scottish Highlands where she watches clouds, pets cows and scribbles stories. In February 2020 she joined the BBC Scottish Voices writer development programme and is currently writing a script. She sits on the board of Northwords Now and reads for the wonderfully wacky Taco Bell Quarterly. Her first published short story was about her Peace Corps experience in Ukraine.

James Northern – James Northern (@JNorthernWrites) is a UK-based writer. His short stories have been published in various anthologies and web journals, including the 2019 and 2020 editions of the National Flash Fiction Day Anthology, the 'Stroud Short Stories Vol.2' anthology, issue 19 of the Riggwelter journal and the 100 Words of Solitude project.

Reshma Ruia – Reshma Ruia is an award winning writer and poet. Her first novel, '*Something Black in the Lentil Soup*', was described in the Sunday Times as 'a gem of straight-faced comedy.' Her second novel manuscript, '*A Mouthful of Silence*' was shortlisted for the SI Leeds Literary Award. Her writing has appeared in The Mechanics' Institute Review, The Nottingham Review, Asia Literary Review, Confluence, Cabinet of Heed,

Funny Pearls, Fictive Dream, The Good Journal, Sguardi Diversi and various anthologies such as *Too Asian Not Asian Enough, No Good Deed, Love across a Broken Map, May We Borrow your Country, Garden Among Fires* and *Mancunian Ways* among others. Her stories have also been commissioned by and broadcast on BBC Radio 4. Her debut collection of poetry, '*A Dinner Party in the Home Counties*,' won the 2019 Word Masala Award. She is the co-founder of The Whole Kahani writers' collective of British South Asian writers.
WWW.RESHMARUIA.COM
Twitter: @RESHMARUIA

Hannah Storm – A journalist for 20 years, Hannah Storm's flash fiction, poetry and creative nonfiction is often inspired by her experiences travelling the world for work. This year she won the 'I Must Be Off!' travel writing prize, placed second in the Bath Flash Fiction Award and was highly commended in the TSS flash prize. She lives in the UK with her family and works as a media consultant and director of a journalism charity.

Rhys Timson – Rhys Timson's stories have appeared in 3:AM Magazine, Litro, Popshot, Structo, Lighthouse and several other journals. His work has also been performed at Liars' League spoken word nights and appeared in Retreat West's *Future Shock* anthology. He lives in

London, where he works as a copy editor. www.rhystimson.com.

Sherri Turner – Sherri Turner has had numerous short stories published in magazines and has won prizes for both poetry and short stories in competitions including the Bristol Prize, the Wells Literary Festival and the Bridport Prize. Her work has also appeared in several anthologies. She tweets at @STurner4077.

Claire Zinkin – Clare Zinkin works as a writer, editor, and children's reading consultant. After training as a journalist, she worked for many years as an editor at a children's publisher before going freelance. She lives in London and is married with three children. She is currently writing her third novel. Website: www.minervareads.com

Enjoyed these short stories and flash fictions?

You can read more of the winning stories from previous year's prizes in the following anthologies:

WHAT WAS LEFT
The winning and shortlisted stories from the 2016 Retreat West Short Story and Flash Fiction Prizes. A past that comes back to haunt a woman when she feels she has no future. A man with no mind of his own living a life of clichés. A teenage girl band that maybe never was. A dying millionaire's bizarre tasks for the family hoping to get his money. A granddaughter losing the grandfather she loves. A list of things about Abraham Lincoln that reveal both sadness and ambition for a modern day schoolgirl. From moving and poignant, to creepy and laugh out loud funny, these stories showcase the talented voices writing short fiction today.

IMPERMANENT FACTS
The winning and shortlisted stories in the 2017 Retreat West Short Story and Flash Fiction Prizes. A woman ventures out into a marsh at night seeking answers about herself that she cannot find; a man enjoys the solitude when his wife goes away for a few days; two young women make a get rich quick plan; and a father longs for the daughter that has gone to teach English in Japan.

These stories and more make up a wonderful collection looking at relationships of all kinds – the ones we have with ourselves, our lovers, our friends and our mothers. They are funny, poignant, sad and strange but all beautifully written and a fine example of the wonderful writers from all around the world that are creating short stories and flash fictions today.

FUTURE SHOCK

The winning and shortlisted stories in the 2018 Retreat West Short Story and Flash Fiction Prizes cross genres, eras and continents to bring you insights into the human condition through many different voices. From a young boy finding his place in the world when watching Magnum PI with his family; to an old woman cooking eggs, inspired by the painting by Velázquez; and a self-styled food cop raiding shops and fast-food outlets not selling what he wants them to. This collection is filled with moments of humour, love and pain. Just like life is. Featuring stories from Joanna Campbell, Manisha Khemka, Richard Buxton, Fiona J. Mackintosh, A.C. Koch, Sherry Morris, James Ellis and more.

http://retreatwestbooks.com

Printed in Great Britain
by Amazon